Learn to Cook
Asian Noodles
& Snacks

Innovative ideas for entertaining with
an Asian flair!

PERIPLUS

Contents

MAIL ORDER SOURCES

Finding the ingredients for Asian home cooking has become very simple. Most supermarkets carry staples such as soy sauce, fresh ginger, and fresh lemongrass. Almost every large metropolitan area has Asian markets serving the local population—just check your local business directory. With the Internet, exotic Asian ingredients and cooking utensils can be easily found online. The following list is a good starting point of online merchants offering a wide variety of goods and services.

http://www.asiafoods.com

http://www.geocities.com/MadisonAvenue/8074/VarorE.html

http://dmoz.org/Shopping/Food/Ethnic_and_Regional/Asian/

http://templeofthai.com/

http://www.orientalpantry.com/

http://www.zestyfoods.com/

http://www.thaigrocer.com/Merchant/index.htm

http://asianwok.com/

http://pilipinomart.com/

http://www.indiangrocerynet.com/

http://www.orientalfoodexpress.com/

Noodle and snack dishes have long been a part of Asia's culinary landscape. Stroll down any street in Asia and you'll almost certainly find food stands, restaurants and food courts packed with customers feasting not just on main courses but also on an almost infinite variety of other mouthwatering noodle and snack dishes.

Noodles and snacks are an important part of Asian homestyle cooking, and because most noodle and snack dishes are easy to prepare and fast to cook, they are perfect for a quick bite or for entertaining guests. They give the host a chance to offer hospitality with a range of delicious treats that, while not intended as a full meal, are substantial dishes in their own right, as the collection of noodle and snack recipes in this book will show.

Noodles play a pivotal role as a snack food and almost every Asian cuisine has its take on the noodle theme. Although rice is a mainstay at the Asian table, rice flour, egg or mung bean noodles are almost as widespread. Asian cooks have taken the noodle and created numerous delectable dishes, from fast stir-fries and healthful salads to invigorating soups and delicate snacks.

The noodle recipes in this book are filling, yet easy to prepare for guests, and the sheer variety of noodles and ingredients on offer mean that you'll be spoilt for choice. Choose from recipes which use a variety of noodles — rice sticks, bean thread and wheat — are prepared in different ways — soups, sauces and stir-fries — use an array of main ingredients — beef, chicken and shrimp to name just a few — and offer a delightful array of tastes ranging from sweet to tangy to spicy.

Asian snacks however, are not limited to just noodles, as anyone familiar with Asian food will tell you. The snack recipes in this volume can be served to complement noodle dishes or other main courses. Choose from numerous savory wraps and rolls, delectable fritters, scrumptious breads and grilled meats and their accompanying dipping sauces.

Whether you're entertaining friends, simply want a quick meal at home or even looking to pack a picnic basket, you can't go wrong with this delicious selection of noodle and snack recipes!

Ingredients Glossary

Banana leaf sheets are used for wrapping rice, meats and a variety of fillings before cooking. The leaves preserve moisture, and also impart a mild fragrance to the food.

Basil exists in three varieties, the most common of which, known in Thailand as *horapa*, has a wonderful aniseed aroma, making it quite different to the common Mediterranean or sweet basil. It has medium to dark green leaves with a purple tinge to the upper stems and purplish flower heads. Lemon-scented basil is often added to soups and salads. Holy basil is stronger in flavor and has purplish markings.

Bok choy is a crunchy, green leafy vegetable that will keep for about one week in a refrigerator, although it tastes best when used fresh. It may be substituted by mustard greens or cabbage.

Carambola is a pale-green acidic fruit about 2–3 in (5–8 cm) long that grows in clusters. Carambola is used whole or sliced to give a sour tang to soups, curries, fish dishes and sambals. Not to be confused with the larger, sweet, five-edged yellow-green starfruit of the same family. Sour grapefruit juice or tamarind juice are good substitutes.

Candlenuts are waxy, cream-colored nuts native to Indonesia. They are similar in size and shape to macadamia nuts, which can be used as a substitute . Candlenuts are ground and used to add texture and a faint flavor to Malay and Nonya dishes. They should not be eaten raw. Store in the refrigerator.

Caraway seeds are small, crescent-shaped seeds often used to flavor baked goods and sometimes curries. Used either whole or ground, caraway seeds should first be toasted in a skillet for a few minutes over low to medium heat to bring out their aroma. Substitute with cumin or anise seeds

Cayenne pepper is a pungent red powder made from ground chili peppers. It is also known as ground red pepper and can be substituted with dried red chili flakes or chili paste.

Chili paste is a bottled sauce made from whole ground chili peppers sold in many grocery stores. To the chilies are generally added a combination of salt, sugar, garlic and sometimes soy beans or ginger. Chili paste comes in many flavors ranging from sweet to spicy.

Chinese sausages or *lap cheong*, are thin, sweet Chinese pork sausages that are delicately perfumed with rice wine. Used as a seasoning rather than eaten on their own, they will keep almost indefinitely without refrigeration.

Coconuts are widely used in Malaysia, Singapore, Sri Lanka, the Philippines, and Indonesia, not just for cooking but also as a source of palm sugar and alcohol. The grated flesh is often added to food and to make **coconut milk**. This is made by blending the freshly grated flesh of a mature coconut with about 1 cup (250 ml) water, and then squeezing the liquid out of it. Coconut milk is very rich and high in cholesterol. Substitute with normal milk. Canned coconut milk is in now widely available in most supermarkets. The thick layer of cream that rises to the top of coconut milk is known as **coconut cream**. It is sold in well-stocked supermarkets and Asian grocery stores.

Coriander is one of the most widely used herbs in Asia. All the parts of this versatile plant — the leaves, seeds and roots — are used in Asian cooking. **Coriander leaves**, also known as cilantro, are widely used as a flavoring and garnish. Fresh coriander leaves have a strong taste and aroma and can be refrigerated in a plastic bag for about one week. Parsley is a suitable substitute. **Coriander seeds** are roasted and ground for use as spice blends in Asian curries. **Coriander roots** are ground and used as a seasoning in Thailand.

Cornstarch is a fine white powder used to thicken gravies, sauces and puddings. It should be mixed with water first before being added to the liquid being thickened, then simmered over low heat until it thickens. Liquids thickened with cornstarch should not be frozen as they tend to turn spongy. Cornstarch is also known as cornflour. It should not be confused with finely ground cornmeal, a yellowish powder which is also known as corn flour.

Fish Sauce or *nam pla* is made from salted, fermented fish or prawns. It is used in Thai and Vietnamese marinades, dressings and dipping sauces. Good quality *nam pla* is golden-brown in color and has a salty, pungent flavor.

Five-spice powder is a Chinese ground spice combination of star anise, Sichuan peppercorns, fennel, cloves and cinnamon. It is used in meat marinades and soup stocks. This mixture is very strong, and should be used in small amounts.

Galangal is a member of the ginger family. It is pinkish or creamy orange-white and has a sharp and pungent taste. It is commonly used in Thai, Malaysian and Indonesian cuisines, and is sold fresh in Asian markets; substitute with ginger. *Garam masala* is an Indian blend of strong aromatic spices used to add flavor and fragrance to curries. Powdered *garam masala* can be bought from Indian or South Asian grocery stores. Store in a jar in the freezer.

Ghee is the rich, delicious clarified butter oil used as the main oil in Indian cooking. It is made from cow or water buffalo milk by removing the milk solids from the oil. It keeps well at room temperature. Substitute with vegetable oil or butter.

Hoisin sauce is a sweet sauce made of soybeans and is used as a dipping sauce and flavoring. Refrigerate after opening.

Kaffir lime is also known as fragrant lime. This citrus fruit has intensely fragrant skin but virtually no juice. The grated skin or rind is added to food.

Kaffir lime leaves are the fragrant leaves of the kaffir lime plant, which are used whole in soups and curries, or shredded finely and added to salads.

Lemongrass is a lemon-scented plant that grows in clumps. Use only the bottom 2–4 in (5–10 cm) portion. If the lemongrass is to be pounded or blended to a paste, discard the outer leaves and use only the pale, tender part. If adding to stews, the stem should be bruised the first. Lemongrass is available in fresh, frozen, dried and powdered forms. About 1 teaspoon of powdered lemongrass is equal to one stalk.

Lentils are protein- and fiber-rich legumes often referred to in Asia by their Indian name, *dal*. Two kinds of lentils are used in this book. **Split chickpeas** or garbanzos (*channa dal*) resemble yellow split peas, which may be used as a substitute. **Black lentils** (*urad dal*) are sold either with their black skin on or husked. Husked black lentils are actually creamy white.

Miso is a salty paste made from fermented soya beans, and is most commonly used in Japanese soups. Various types of *Miso* are available, with the two most common being white and red *miso*. White *miso* has a lighter flavor than red *miso* as it is less salty. Miso is readily available from Japanese grocery stores and well stocked supermarkets.

Mushrooms are prized in Asian cooking for the flavor and texture they add to dishes. *Shiitake* or Chinese black mushrooms are generally large and meaty, and are used in soups, stir-fries and side dishes, or even as a meat substitute. Substitute with porcini mushrooms. Fresh *shiitake* are increasingly available in supermarkets. Fresh, delicately sheathed **straw mushrooms** are excellent in soups and vegetable dishes. **Button mushrooms** and large, bland **oyster mushrooms** are good for stir-frying. *Enokitaki* (**golden mushrooms**) are clusters of slender, stalks with tiny caps, and are available fresh and tinned. The tough ends of the *enokitaki* should be discarded before use.

Noodles are widely used in Asian cooking. They generally come in different widths ranging from fine vermicelli-like noodles to broad, flat noodles. Dried Asian noodles can be found in most supermarkets. Fresh Asian noodles are more easily found in Asian grocery stores or markets. **Dried egg noodles** are made from egg, wheat flour and water and are sold in thin or medium thicknesses. **Laksa noodles** are rice noodles that resemble white spaghetti. They are used in *laksa*, a noodle dish popular in Southeast Asia. **Mung bean** or **glass noodles** are thin, transparent noodles made from mung beans. They readily absorb other flavors in a dish. Substitute with rice vermicelli or angel hair pasta. **Rice noodles** are made with rice flour and water, and sold as **rice sticks**, vermicelli or rice threads. **Wheat noodles** are made from wheat flour, water, and sometimes eggs.

Oyster sauce is a thick sauce made from ground oysters, water, salt, cornflour and caramel coloring. It is often used in Chinese cooking to intensify the flavor of the food. It is often splashed onto stir-fried vegetables and meat, and sometimes added to marinades. Oyster sauce should be refrigerated after opening.

Palm sugar is made from the refined sap of the sugar palm. Available in Asian grocery stores, it is usually sold in small disks that are $1/_2$-in (1-cm) thick and 3-in ($7^1/_2$-cm) wide, or are sometimes sold in larger cellophane-wrapped blocks. Palm sugar may be substituted with dark brown sugar or maple syrup.

Plum sauce is a reddish-brown condiment made from salted plums, chilies, vinegar and sugar. Sold in tins and jars in Asian grocery stores and well stocked supermarkets, plum sauce should be refrigerated after opening.

Red chili oil is a fragrant spicy seasoning used to enliven some Sichuanese dishes. The oil is flavored by cooking it with dried chilies or chili powder. The oil is then simmered until the chilies turn dark brown, then strained.

Rice paper wrappers are used for wrapping spring rolls and various grilled meats and leafy greens. They are made from ground rice, water and salt and dried in the sun. They should be moistened before use by dipping in water or by covering with a moist cloth until soft. Sold at Asian markets and grocery stores, rice paper wrappers do vary in quality, so look for packages in which the sheets are not split or crumbled.

Salam **leaves** are large, dark green leaves added to curries. Rarely encountered outside Indonesia, the *salam* leaf has no direct substitute and may be omitted if not available.

Salted radish keeps almost indefinitely on the shelf, and is often added to rice porridge (congee) and other dishes. Salted radish keeps almost indefinitely on the shelf, and is often added to rice porridge (congee) and other dishes.

Sesame seeds are small and pear-shaped and come in several colors — white, yellow, brown or black — and are white on the inside when hulled. Sesame seeds are toasted and crushed to make **sesame paste**. The paste can be quite hard and should be mixed with a little sesame oil or water to make it into a smooth paste. Sesame paste should not be confused with the sweet sesame paste that is made from black sesame seeds and used in some cakes and desserts. It may be substituted with Middle Eastern tahini mixed with sesame oil to give it a more pronounced flavor.

Shrimp paste, comes in two forms, dried and wet. **Dried shrimp paste**, also known as *trassi* or *belacan*, is a dense mixture of fermented, ground shrimp used extensively in Southeast Asian cooking. There are many different types, ranging in color from pink to blackish brown. The pink-colored paste is good for curry pastes, while the darker, blackish-brown paste is used for making dipping sauces. Shrimp paste should be cooked before eating; if the recipe you are using does not call for it to be fried together with other ingredients, either grill or dry-fry the shrimp paste before pounding. To grill, wrap a piece of the paste in a piece of foil and toast under a grill or dry-fry in a pan for about 2 minutes on each side. **Wet shrimp paste** is also known as *hae ko* or *petis*. It is sold in jars and may be added to recipes straight from the jar.

Sichuan pepper-salt powder is made by toasting Sichuan peppercorns and salt in a skillet over low to medium heat until fragrant. Also available commercially in Asian grocery stores.

Soy sauce is fermented from soya beans and salt, and is commonly used in marinades, sauces and dips. Two different types are widely used in Asian cooking. **Thick soy sauce** is often added to give a dark coloring and strong, smoky flavor to a dish. **Light soy sauce** is thinner, lighter in color and saltier than black soy sauce. Low salt varieties are also available. Poor-quality soy sauce can ruin the taste of even the best food, so it's well worth spending a bit more for higher-grade soy sauce.

Spring roll wrappers are thin sheets of rice flour dough used to enclose a variety of fillings such as meats and vegetables. The wrappers are usually rolled into a cigar shape and deep-fried until golden brown. Spring roll wrappers are sold frozen in supermarkets, and should be defrosted and separated before use. The defrosted wrappers should be covered by a damp kitchen towel while the spring rolls are being prepared.

Star anise is a dark brown, strongly-flavored spice that resembles an eight-pointed star. Its aroma is similar to that of anise or cinnamon. Star anise should be stored in a tightly-sealed jar in a cool, dry place to preserve its aroma.

Tamarind pulp comes from the pods of the tamarind tree. It is usually sold in cellophane-wrapped squares or jars with the seeds removed and the flesh compressed. The pulp is the key ingredient in **tamarind juice**, a sour liquid that adds intense flavor to many Asian dishes. To make tamarind juice, soak 3 tablespoons of tamarind pulp in $1^1/_2$ cups (375 ml) warm water for 20 minutes. Squeeze the pulp, stir the mixture well, then strain the mixture and discard the solids.

Tapioca flour is used as a thickener in doughs and pie fillings and sometimes in soups and stews as well. Tapioca flour does not become spongy when frozen and also imparts a chewier texture to baked goods.

Tapioca pearls are made from cassava roots. The round, pellet-sized pearls are often used to thicken doughs and are usually soaked in warm water before use.

Tofu (bean curd) is available firm or soft. **Firm tofu** stays in shape when cut or cooked and has a stronger, slightly sour taste. **Soft tofu** is slippery and tends to crumble easily but has a more silky texture and refined flavor. **Tofu skin** is the thin rich layer of soy protein that forms on the surface of soy bean milk while it is being boiled to make tofu. The dried variety, or **tofu sheet**, is available in most Asian grocery stores. It has the same nutritional benefits and is easier to work with in the kitchen, although it is less tasty than tofu skin. Tofu sheet is commonly used in stir-fries and vegetarian cooking as a meat substitute.

Torch ginger buds, known as *bunga kantan* or *bunga siantan* in Malaysia, and *kaalaa* in Thailand, are eaten raw with a dip, added to salads or cooked in soups and curries. There is no substitute for this; if you are able to obtain the fresh buds, freeze whole for future use.

Water convolvulus is also known as water spinach, morning glory and by its Malay name *kangkung*. This aquatic plant is rich in protein and minerals such as iron. The arrowhead-shaped leaves and tips are usually stir-fried.

Wonton skins are square wrappers that come in various sizes and thicknesses. They are often filled with meat, then steamed, fried or used in soups.

Yellow bean paste is a salty brown sauce made from fermented soy beans, and is available in cans or jars. If you buy it in a can, transfer it into a jar. It can then be stored indefinitely in the refrigerator.

Condiments, Sauces and Dips

The following dips, pastes, sauces and side dishes are either recipes in their own right or basic components of other recipes featured later in this book.

Sweet and Spicy Plum or Apricot Sauce

$1/2$ cup (125 ml) water
1 cup (200 g) sugar
$1/2$ cup (125 ml) vinegar
1 fresh red chili, finely chopped
3 cloves garlic, peeled and finely chopped
2 tablespoons Japanese apricot or Chinese plum sauce (apricot jam or marmalade may also be used)

1 Combine the water, sugar and vinegar in a small saucepan. Bring to the boil over high heat, then reduce the heat to low. Cook until the mixture begins to thicken, about 40 minutes.
2 Add the red chili, garlic and apricot or plum sauce. Stir a few times. Remove from the heat and cool before serving.

Sweet and Spicy Peanut Sauce

$1/4$ cup (60 ml) water
$1/2$ cup (100 g) sugar
1 teaspoon salt
$1/4$ cup (60 ml) vinegar
$1/2$ teaspoon minced fresh red chili
$1/4$ cup (45 g) roasted ground peanuts

1 Bring the water, sugar and salt to a boil in a saucepan.
2 Reduce the heat to low and simmer for about 15 minutes.
3 Remove from the heat. Stir in the vinegar and minced chili. Let cool and add the peanuts before serving.

Tamarind Juice

3 tablespoons dried tamarind pulp
$1 1/2$ cups (375 ml) warm water

1 Soak the tamarind pulp in warm water for 20 minutes.
2 Squeeze the pulp with your fingers and stir well. Strain the mixture and discard the solids.

Red Curry Paste

1 tablespoon coriander
  seeds
3 dried chilies, soaked
  30 minutes
1 stalk lemon grass,
  thinly sliced
3 thin slices galangal
3 shallots, peeled and
  roughly chopped
7 cloves garlic
1 teaspoon kaffir lime
  rind, grated
1 teaspoon shrimp paste
$1/_3$ cup (90 ml) water, or
  more as needed

1 Roast the coriander seeds in a dry frying-pan over medium heat until fragrant, about 2 minutes. Combine all the ingredients in a blender and process until smooth.

2 Store unused portions in an airtight container. Leftovers keep well in the refrigerator or freezer.

Cucumber Salad

2 tablespoons sugar
1 teaspoon salt
$1/_3$ cup (90 ml) warm
  water
2 tablespoons vinegar
3 shallots, thinly sliced
1 fresh red chili, seeded
  and sliced
1 cucumber, peeled,
  quartered lengthwise
  and thinly sliced

1 Dissolve the sugar and salt in the water. Add the vinegar.

2 Place the shallots and the chili slices on top of the cucumber in a serving bowl. Pour the sugar water mixture over the top.

Seasoned Sliced Chilies

10–15 small chilies,
  finely sliced
2 tablespoons light soy
  sauce
2 tablespoons fresh lime
  juice

1 Combine the chilies, soy sauce and lime juice in a small bowl. Alternatively use 1–2 red or green chilies sliced thinly.

Vietnamese Fish Sauce Dip

1 teaspoon chili paste,
  or 3 fresh red chilies,
  seeded and chopped
3 cloves garlic, peeled
  and finely chopped
1/4 cup (60 g) sugar
3 tablespoons fresh lime
  juice
1 tablespoon vinegar
3 tablespoons fish sauce
1/2 cup (125 ml) water
1/2 teaspoon salt

1 Combine all the ingredients in a bowl and mix well. Serve in small dipping bowls, one per person.

Makes 1 cup (250 ml)
Preparation time: **10 mins**

Spicy-sweet Thai Dip

1/4 cup (30 g) onions,
  thinly sliced
1 tablespoon lemon
  grass, thinly sliced
1 tablespoon fresh
  ginger, grated
1/2 tablespoon shrimp
  paste
1/2 cup (90 g) fresh
  grated coconut
1/4 cup (30 g) dried
  shrimps
1 1/2 teaspoons salt
2 cups (500 ml) plus
  1/2 to 3/4 cups
  (125 to 180 ml) water
1 1/4 cups (200 g) palm
  sugar
Crushed peanuts for
  garnish

1 Roast the onions, lemon grass, ginger and shrimp paste on a flat baking sheet in the oven at 250°F (120°C) until golden, about 15 minutes. Roast the coconut at 350°F (180°C) until golden brown, stirring often, about 10 minutes.
2 Put the onions, lemon grass, ginger, shrimp paste, coconut, dried shrimps and salt into a blender and add 1/2 cup (125 ml) water gradually and process, adding more water if necessary. Process for a few seconds; the consistency does not need to be smooth.
3 Transfer the mixture to a large saucepan and add 2 cups (500 ml) water and the palm sugar. Bring the mixture to the boil over medium heat, then reduce the heat to medium-low and cook for 1 hour and 15 minutes, stirring occasionally. Remove from the heat and cool.

Preparation time: **15 mins**
Cooking time: **1 hour 45 mins**

Sweet-sour Chili Dip

4 fresh red or green-
  chilis, sliced
2 tablespoons vinegar
Sugar to taste

1 Combine the chili and vinegar in a small bowl, then add sugar to taste.

Vietnamese Peanut Sauce

1 1/2 cups (375 ml) water
1/2 cup (125 ml) hoisin
  sauce
1/2 cup (125 ml)
  tamarind juice
1/2 cup (120 g) crunchy
  peanut butter
3 tablespoons sugar
1/2 cup (100 g) ground
  peanuts
2 tablespoons garlic,
  minced

1 Mix all the ingredients in a bowl and stir well.

Makes 3 1/2 cups (875 ml)
Preparation time: **10 mins**
Cooking time: **5 mins**

Shrimp Paste Dip (*Hae Ko*)

2 tablespoons shrimp
  paste (*hae ko* or *petis*)
2 tablespoons hot water

1 Combine the shrimp paste dip and water and serve in small dipping bowls, one per person.

Vietnamese Caramel Sauce

1/3 cup (80 g) sugar
1/4 cup (70 ml) fish sauce
4 shallots, peeled and
  sliced
1/4 teaspoon freshly
  ground black pepper

Makes 1/3 cups (85 ml)
Preparation time: **5 mins**
Cooking time: **10 mins**

1 Cook the sugar in a saucepan over low heat until it starts to melt and caramelize. Remove the pan from the heat and add the fish sauce.
2 Return the pan to the heat and bring to a boil. Stir often to prevent the sugar mixture from scorching. Cook until the mixture turns syrupy, about 4 minutes. Add the black pepper and shallots and stir well. Remove the pan from the heat and let the sauce cool.

Basic Chicken Stock

1 chicken carcass or 1 lb (450 g) chicken bones
4 ginger slices
10 peppercorns
8 cups (2 liters) water

1 Rinse chicken carcass or bones thoroughly, discarding any blood clots and fat.
2 Place in a large saucepan and add ginger slices, peppercorns and water. Bring to the boil, skimming off any scum that rises. Allow stock to simmer on low heat for 1 hour, until the liquid is reduced to roughly 4 cups (1 liter). Strain and discard the solids.

Crispy Fried Shallots (used as garnish)

$1/2$ cup (125 ml) oil
6–8 shallots, peeled and thinly sliced

1 Heat oil in a saucepan over medium heat and fry the sliced shallots until golden brown, taking great care not to over-brown them as this makes them taste bitter. Carefully remove fried shallots with a slotted spoon, transferring them onto a plate lined with paper towels. If not using them immediately, store in a dry, airtight jar to preserve their crispness.

Scallion Oil or Garlic Oil

$1/4$ cup (60 ml) oil
2 scallions, thinly sliced or 2 tablespoons garlic, minced

1 Heat $1/4$ cup oil over medium heat in a small saucepan. Remove the saucepan from the heat and add the scallion or garlic. Let the mixture cool to room temperature and store in a tightly sealed jar where it will stay fresh for up to one week.

Roasted Rice Powder

$1/2$ cup (120 g) uncooked long-grain or glutinous rice

1 Spread $1/2$ cup (120 g) raw long-grain or glutinous rice on a baking sheet and bake, stirring often, in a 500°F (250°C) oven until the rice turns brown. Alternatively, spread the rice out in an oil-free skillet and cook over medium-low heat, stirring often, until it browns and becomes fragrant. Remove the rice from the heat and grind in a blender until the grains resemble crushed black peppercorns. Stores well in a tightly sealed container for several months.

Sweet Lime Chutney

1 lb (450 g) limes, seeded and finely chopped
2 tablespoons salt
1 1/2 cups (150 g) onions, chopped
2 tablespoons mustard seeds, roasted and coarsely ground
1 1/4 cups (300 g) sugar
1 1/2 cups (300 ml) white vinegar
2 teaspoons cayenne pepper
1 teaspoon ground turmeric
3/4 cup (100 g) raisins

1 Place the chopped lime pieces into a ceramic or glass bowl. Sprinkle with salt and mix well. Transfer to a stainless steel saucepan, add the remaining ingredients and stir well.
2 Cook over low heat until the lime pieces become tender and the chutney thickens, about 1 1/4 hours.

Serves 6
Preparation time: **15 mins**
Cooking time: **1 hour 15 mins**

Sweet-sour Tomato Chutney

2 tablespoons oil
1/2 teaspoon black lentils (*urad dal*)
1/2 teaspoon mustard
1/2 teaspoon cumin
1/2 teaspoon fennel seeds
1 bay leaf
1/2 cup (125 ml) tamarind juice (see page 6)
2 cups (80 g) ripe tomatoes, diced
1 cup (200 g) sugar
1 fresh red chili, finely sliced
1 cup (120 g) pitted dates, quartered
3/4 teaspoon salt

1 Heat the oil and fry the black lentils, spices and the bay leaf until aromatic.
2 Add in the remaining ingredients, bring to a boil, then lower the heat and simmer until the chutney thickens, about 45 minutes.

Black lentils are sold either with their black skin on or husked. Husked black lentils are creamy white in color.

Serves 6
Preparation time: **10 mins**
Cooking time: **45 mins**

Coconut Mango Chutney

1 1/4 cups (200 g) unripe mango, peeled and diced
2 1/2 cups (240 g) fresh grated coconut
4 green chilies, seeded and cut into 1/2-in (1-cm) lengths
1/2 teaspoon salt
1 1/2 tablespoons oil
1/2 teaspoon black lentils (urad dal)
1/2 teaspoon mustard seeds
1 sprig curry leaves

1 In a food processor or blender, coarsely grind the diced mango, coconut, green chilies and salt. Set aside.
2 Heat the oil in a small saucepan over medium heat and fry the black gram until golden brown. Add the mustard seeds and curry leaves and fry until the seeds pop. Stir in the asafoetida and remove from the heat.
3 Add the black gram and fried spices to the ground fruit.

Serves 6
Preparation time: 10 mins
Cooking time: 10 mins

Coconut and Coriander Leaf Chutney

5 cups (500 g) grated coconut
1 2/3 cups (100 g) fresh coriander leaves (cilantro), chopped
4 green chilies, seeded and sliced
4 tablespoons lime juice
3 slices fresh ginger
1 teaspoon salt
1/2 cup (125 ml) water

1 Place all the ingredients in a food processor and blend until smooth.

Serves 6
Preparation time: 20 mins
Cooking time: nil

Four types of Indian chutney in a typical serving tray.

Fresh Chinese Spring Rolls

2 sweet Chinese sausages
  (*lap cheong*)
1 tablespoon oil
2 eggs, lightly beaten
8 spring roll wrappers
1 baby cucumber, peeled
  and cut into strips
8 oz (225 g) firm tofu,
  cut into thin strips
8 scallions, trimmed
1 cup (250 g) cooked
  crabmeat, leave some
  for garnish
$1/2$ lb (225 g) bean
  sprouts, blanched for
  2 minutes

Sauce
1 cup (250 ml) Basic
  Chicken Stock (see
  page 13) or water
$1/3$ cup (50 g) palm sugar
$1/4$ cup (60 ml) tamarind
  juice (see page 9)
$1/2$ cup (90 g) roasted
  peanuts, finely ground
2 tablespoons Crispy Fried
  Shallots (see page 13)
1 tablespoon fish sauce
1 tablespoon thick sweet
  soy sauce (see note)
1 tablespoon oyster sauce
1 teaspoon salt
4 teaspoons tapioca flour
  or cornstarch mixed
  with $1/4$ cup (60 ml)
  water
$1/4$ teaspoon five-spice
  powder
$1/4$ cup (45 g) toasted
  sesame seeds

1 Steam the Chinese sausages for 5 to 6 minutes, cool and cut into 8 thin strips lengthwise.

2 Heat the oil in a wok or skillet over medium heat and fry the eggs into an omelet. Cut the omelet into 8 long pieces and set aside.

3 Place a spring roll wrapper on a flat surface and put a piece of sausage, omelet, cucumber, tofu, scallion, 2 tablespoons of crabmeat and some bean sprouts on the wrapper. Roll the wrapper up tightly. Repeat until you use all the wrappers.

4 To make the Sauce, combine all the ingredients, except the sesame seeds, in a saucepan. Cook over medium heat until the mixture boils; stir a few times. Add the sesame seeds when the mixture begins to thicken. Transfer to a serving dish.

5 Serve rolls as they are, or steam the rolls for 1 to 2 minutes in a steamer or microwave oven. Garnish each roll with some crabmeat and serve the Sauce on the side or drizzle over top.

Thick sweet soy sauce is not widely available in the West but can be approximated by adding $1/2$ teaspoon dark brown sugar to 1 tablespoon of normal thick soy sauce. Hoisin Sauce is a good substitute.

Serves 8
Preparation time: **20 mins**
Assembling time: **20 mins**

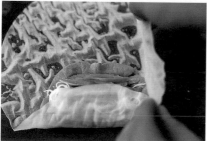

Fold the bottom portion of rice paper over the filling; then fold the two sides in.

Place two halves of shrimp side by side, then continue folding the spring roll.

Vietnamese Shrimp and Pork Salad Rolls

These rolls are a Vietnamese shrimp and pork salad wrapped in rice paper. The aromatic herbs in the rolls lend a refreshing taste. If you are looking for a picnic snack food, these rolls are perfect! The traditional filling calls for pork and shrimp but you can also use sausage or egg. Tofu slices or avocado can also be used to make a delicious vegetarian version.

¹/₄ lb (110 g) dried rice vermicelli noodles
¹/₂ lb (225 g) lean pork
3 cups (750 ml) water
2 scallions, sliced in half
¹/₂ lb (225 g) medium shrimps
1 baby cucumber, quartered and thinly sliced
1 carrot, peeled and grated
6 large Boston lettuce leaves, stem ends removed and halved
2 sprigs fresh coriander leaves (cilantro), coarsely chopped
12 sheets rice paper
Vietnamese Peanut Sauce (see page 12)

Serves 4–6
Preparation time: 30 mins
Cooking time: 25 mins

1 Soak the vermicelli in cold water for 20 minutes. Blanch in boiling water then rinse under cold water. Drain well and set aside on a plate.

2 Meanwhile, heat water in saucepan and bring to a boil over medium heat. Add the pork and scallions and cook for 20 minutes. Remove the pork from the saucepan and when it is cool enough to handle, slice into thin strips. Set aside on a serving plate.

3 In the same water, cook the shrimps for 2 minutes. Remove and cool in ice water, peel and cut in half lengthwise. Set aside with the pork. Discard the scallions.

4 Arrange the cucumber, carrot, lettuce leaves and fresh coriander on a big platter.

5 Sprinkle water lightly on 2 sheets of rice paper at a time and when each softens and is pliable, place a piece of lettuce on one half of the rice paper. Put 1 piece pork, 1 small clump noodles and pieces of cucumber and carrot on top. Fold the bottom portion over the filling, fold in the right and left sides and roll the wrapper one more time so that it is two-thirds rolled.

6 Place 2 halves shrimp end to end along the top of the roll and place several fresh coriander leaves on top. Roll the wrapper tightly until the edges seal shut. Place the finished rolls on a plate and cover with a damp towel to keep them moist until serving time. Repeat with the remaining ingredients. Serve with the Vietnamese Peanut Sauce.

Crispy Thai Fried Spring Rolls

1 lb (450 g) ground pork or chicken
3¹/₂ oz (100 g) dried bean thread noodles,
2 mushrooms, soaked and stems removed
2 cups (200 g) green cabbage, shredded
2 cups (220 g) bean sprouts, blanched and roughly chopped
1 carrot, grated
2 cloves garlic, finely chopped
2 tablespoons fresh coriander leaves (cilantro), chopped
2 tablespoons fish sauce (page 10)
1 tablespoon light soy sauce
1 teaspoon salt
1 teaspoon ground white pepper
1 large egg
24 spring roll wrappers
1 tablespoon cornstarch mixed with enough water to form paste
3 cups (750 ml) oil
1 cup (250 ml) Sweet and Spicy Peanut Sauce (see page 9)

1 Soak the bean thread noodles in water for 30 minutes, drain in a colander and cut into 2-in (5-cm) lengths.
2 Combine all the ingredients except the wrappers, cornstarch paste and oil in a mixing bowl. Lay a spring roll wrapper on a flat surface and place 2 tablespoons of the filling on the lower half of the wrapper. Fold the bottom edge of the wrapper over the filling. Next, fold the right and left edges over the first fold, then roll tightly. Seal the edge of roll with the cornstarch paste. Repeat until the wrappers and filling are finished.
3 Heat the oil in a wok over high heat. Place the rolls, a few at a time, into the oil and deep-fry until golden brown. Remove with a slotted spoon or tongs. Drain on paper towels. Serve hot with Sweet and Spicy Peanut Sauce.

Makes 24 rolls
Preparation time: 30 min + 30 mins soaking
Cooking time: 20 mins

Thai-style Egg Salad

12 pieces leaf or butterhead lettuce
6 hard-boiled eggs, shelled and thinly sliced
2 small shallots, thinly sliced
$1/2$ cup (20 g) Chinese celery or Italian parsley,
  chopped
$1/4$ cup (25 g) Crispy Fried Shallots (see page 13)
2 tablespoons fried garlic
1 sprig fresh coriander leaves (cilantro), coarsely
  chopped

Dressing
1 tablespoons Thai chili paste (*nam prik pao*)
2 tablespoons soy sauce
2 tablespoons fresh lime juice
1 teaspoons sugar

1 Line a serving platter with the lettuce leaves. Place
the egg slices on the leaves and sprinkle with the
shallots, Chinese celery, fried shallots, fried garlic, and
fresh coriander.
2 Combine the dressing ingredients and pour over the
salad just before serving.

Serves 4–6
Preparation time: **20 mins**
Cooking time: **5 mins**

Vietnamese Pork and Shrimp Crêpe

3 tablespoons oil
$1/2$ cup (100 g) onion, thinly sliced
2 scallions, finely chopped
$1/2$ lb (225 g) bean sprouts
$1/2$ lb (225 g) mushrooms, thinly sliced
10–20 Boston lettuce leaves, rinsed and trimmed
1 cup (40 g) fresh mint leaves, rinsed
8 sprigs fresh coriander leaves (cilantro), rinsed
1 baby cucumber, peeled and thinly sliced
$2^1/2$ cups (625 ml) Vietnamese Fish Sauce Dip (see page 11)

Filling
$1/2$ lb (225 g) lean pork, thinly sliced
$1/2$ lb (225 g) shrimps cleaned and deveined
$1/2$ teaspoon salt
$1/2$ teaspoon sugar
1 tablespoon fish sauce
4 cloves garlic, minced

Batter
1 cup (100 g) rice flour
1 cup (250 ml) cold water
1 cup (250 ml) coconut milk
$1/2$ teaspoon salt
$1/4$ teaspoon turmeric

1 To make the Filling, combine the pork, shrimps, salt, sugar, fish sauce and garlic in a large mixing bowl and mix well. Set aside.

2 To make the Batter, combine the rice flour, water, coconut milk, salt and turmeric in a large mixing bowl. Set aside.

3 Heat 2 tablespoons oil in a wok over high heat. Sauté the onion slices until soft. Add the Filling mixture and stir-fry for 2 to 3 minutes or until the pork loses its pink color and the shrimps turns pink. Remove from the heat and set aside.

4 Heat 1 tablespoon oil in a wok or a medium nonstick skillet over medium heat until very hot. Stir the Batter well and pour $1/3$ cup (90 ml) into the wok. Quickly tilt the pan around to spread the mixture into a thin pancake.

5 Scatter a handful of scallions, bean sprouts and mushrooms, 2 to 3 pieces of pork and 2 shrimps on the lower half of the pancake. Reduce the heat to low and cover the pan. Cook for 3 to 4 minutes or until the pancake browns and turns crispy.

6 Fold the pancake in half and slide onto a platter. Keep warm in a 200°F (100°C) oven.

7 Repeat the procedure until the Batter is used up, making 7 or 8 more pancakes.

8 Before serving, wrap a portion of the pancake in a lettuce leaf with the mint leaves, fresh coriander leaves and cucumber. Serve with the Vietnamese Fish Sauce Dip.

Makes 8 pancakes
Preparation time: **30 mins**
Cooking time: **40 mins**

Thai Lettuce Leaf Cups

The trick to enjoying this traditional Thai snack is in sampling a bit of everything in the leaf cup — the combined flavors and textures make this a real treat. Serve with Spicy-sweet Thai Dip.

1 lime or lemon, peeled and finely diced
2 in (5 cm) fresh ginger, peeled and diced
1 shallot, peeled and diced
$^1/_4$ cup (30 g) tiny dried shrimps or meat jerky or salami or dried sausage, finely diced
1 tablespoon fresh chilies, thinly sliced
$^1/_4$ cup (45 g) roasted unsalted peanuts, skins removed
$^1/_4$ cup (40 g) roasted coconut
10 small pieces Chinese mustard greens or leaf lettuce or *bok choy* leaves(about 150 g)
1 cup (250 ml) Spicy-sweet Thai Dip (see page 11)

1 Arrange the leaf cup ingredients in separate piles on a serving tray. Add crushed peanuts to the Spicy-sweet Thai Dip and serve in a small dish.

2 To serve, make a triangular cone from a leaf and fill the cone with 1 teaspoon coconut. Add 1 piece of each of the other ingredients. Spoon $^1/_2$ teaspoon Spicy-sweet Thai Dip over the contents and fold the leaf over to cover the filling before eating.

Serves 12
Preparation and cooking time: **2 hours**

Tapioca Balls with Pork Filling

2 cups (300 g) tapioca pearls
1 cup (250 ml) warm water
$1/4$ cup (30 g) diced salted radish
3 fresh coriander roots
4 cloves garlic, peeled
$1/2$ teaspoon whole black peppercorns
2 tablespoons oil
1 cup (180 g) ground pork
1 cup (100 g) diced shallots or onion
$1/2$ cup (75 g) palm sugar
$1/4$ cup (60 ml) fish sauce
$1/2$ cup (90 g) ground roasted peanuts
4 tablespoons garlic oil
10 cups ($2^1/2$ liters) water
2 tablespoons fried garlic, as garnish
1 head leaf lettuce, leaves separated and rinsed
9 sprigs fresh coriander leaves

Makes 60
Preparation time: **50 mins**
Cooking time: **20 mins**

1 Combine the tapioca pearls and warm water in a mixing bowl and stir with a wooden spoon until mixed. Knead into a soft dough. Cover with a moist cloth and set aside.

2 Wash the salted radish, squeeze dry and set aside. Using a pestle and mortar, pound the coriander roots, garlic and peppercorns until fine.

3 Heat the 2 tablespoons oil over medium heat in a wok. Cook the pounded mixture until fragrant, about 3 minutes. Add the pork and keep stirring, breaking up any lumps. Add the onion and salted radish. Stir in the palm sugar and fish sauce and continue to cook until the liquid is almost evaporated. Add the peanuts. Stir until the filling mixture thickens. Remove from the heat and cool.

4 To make the balls, dip your hands in cold water. Take about 1 teaspoon tapioca dough and shape it into a small ball, then flatten it. Place 1 teaspoon filling in the center and gather the edges up to form a ball. Repeat to use up the remaining dough and filling.

5 Use the garlic oil to oil a serving platter. Bring the 10 cups ($2^1/2$ liters) water to the boil in a large saucepan. Drop the tapioca balls into the water, about 10 pieces at a time. When they float to the surface, use a slotted spoon to scoop them out, place them on the serving platter and sprinkle with the fried garlic. Alternatively, steam the balls over high heat for 5 minutes. Serve with the lettuce leaves and fresh coriander for wrapping.

Steamed Shrimp Dumplings

30 circular wonton skins
3 tablespoons Garlic Oil
(see page 12)
$^1/_4$ cup (60 ml) Chili
Vinegar Sauce (see
page 12)
$1^1/_2$ in ($3^1/_2$ cm) fresh
ginger, julienned

Filling
3 cloves garlic
3 fresh coriander roots
10 whole black
peppercorns
$^1/_3$ lb (150 g) ground
pork (about 1 cup)
$^1/_3$ lb (150 g) shrimp,
chopped (about 1 cup)
$^1/_2$ cup onion, chopped
6 water chestnuts,
peeled and diced
1 tablespoon corn starch
1 tablespoon sugar
1 teaspoon fish sauce
1 teaspoon light soy
sauce
$^1/_2$ teaspoon salt

1 To make the Filling, grind the garlic, coriander roots and peppercorns until fine. Combine this paste with the remaining Filling ingredients in a mixing bowl until well blended.

2 Working with 1 skin at a time, place 1 heaped teaspoon of the Filling in the center of the skin and gather the sides of the wrapper around the Filling, forming natural pleats. As you work, press on the Filling to pack it tightly.

3 Tap each dumpling lightly to flatten the bottom and make it stand upright. Place the dumplings in a steamer basket over boiling water, cover and steam over high heat for 5 minutes. Brush the tops with Garlic Oil. Remove from the heat to a serving platter. To eat, dip in Chili Vinegar Sauce and julienned ginger.

Makes 30 dumplings
Preparation time: 30 mins
Cooking time: 5 mins

Place 1 heaped teaspoon of filling in the center of each wonton skin.

Gather the sides of the wrapper around the filling, forming natural pleats.

Vietnamese Pork and Crab Spring Rolls

Almost everyone loves the classic Vietnamese spring rolls or *cha gio* (pronounced "cha yoh"). These take a little time to prepare, but are worth the effort. Look for rice paper wrappers in well-stocked Asian markets.

24 sheets rice paper
  wrappers
2 cups (500 ml) oil for
  deep-frying
10–20 Boston lettuce
  leaves
1 cup (40 g) fresh
  mint leaves
1 cup (40 g) fresh
  coriander leaves
1 baby cucumber, peeled
  and cut into thin strips
2 1/2 cups (625 ml)
  Vietnamese Fish Sauce
  Dip (page 11)

Filling
2 oz (60 g) dried bean
  thread noodles
1/2 lb (225 g) lean
  ground pork
3/4 cup (95 g) crab meat,
  picked clean
1/2 cup (100 g) onion,
  diced
2 scallions, finely chopped
1 carrot, grated
1/4 lb (110 g) bean
  sprouts, blanched
  and drained
1 teaspoon salt
1 tablespoon fish sauce
1 large egg, beaten lightly
1/2 teaspoon freshly
  ground black pepper

1 To make the Filling, soak the bean thread noodles in cold water for 20 minutes. Drain and cut into 2-in (5-cm) sections. In a large mixing bowl, combine the noodles, with the other Filling ingredients and mix together well.

2 Sprinkle 1 sheet rice paper lightly with water and when each softens and is pliable, put 2 tablespoons of Filling mixture along one edge of the paper. Fold the top edge of the rice paper over the Filling, then the right and left sides, continue to roll lengthwise until it forms a packet. Repeat procedure with rice paper until you have used up the Filling. You should have approximately 24 rolls.

3 Heat the oil in a skillet over medium heat. Fry the rolls, a few at a time, until crisp and golden on all sides. Do not overcook. Remove from the oil and drain on paper towels.

4 To serve, wrap each roll in a lettuce leaf with mint leaves, fresh coriander leaves and a few strips of cucumber. Serve with the Vietnamese Fish Sauce Dip for dipping.

Serves 4–6
Preparation time: **45 mins**
Cooking time: **20 mins**

Fold the bottom edge over the filling then fold in the sides.

Roll the spring roll away from you, keeping the edges folded in, until paper is finished.

Chicken and Shrimp in an Egg Net

3 tablespoons oil
2 cloves garlic, chopped
1 teaspoon fresh
  coriander root or
  stems, chopped
1 teaspoon freshly
  ground black pepper
$1/2$ lb (225 g) shrimps,
  shelled, deveined and
  minced
1 lb (450 g) chicken,
  minced
1 teaspoon salt
2 tablespoons palm
  sugar, crumbled
1 tablespoon shallots,
  chopped
4 tablespoons ground
  peanuts
2 eggs
2 teaspoons fresh
  coriander leaves
  (cilantro), chopped
4 fresh red chilies, thinly
  sliced

1 Heat oil in a wok over medium heat and sauté the garlic, coriander root and black pepper for 2 minutes, or until fragrant.
2 Add the shrimp and chicken and continue stirring until almost cooked, 2 to 3 minutes. Add salt, palm sugar, shallots and peanuts, stirring for a further minute. Transfer the mixture to a bowl and set aside.
3 Beat the eggs in a separate bowl. Make a cone from a piece of waxed or parchment paper, pour a small amount of the eggs into the cone. and squeeze the egg into a heated nonstick pan or crêpe pan, shaping it into a square net, about 4 x 4 in (10 x 10 cm). Carefully remove from pan with a spatula.
4 When cool enough to handle, place a small amount of coriander leaves and chili slices in the center of the egg net. Put 2 teaspoons of the mixture on top and fold the sides toward the center. Fold in the remaining sides, so that it resembles a small square package. Serve immediately.
5 A simple alternative to the egg nest is to prepare a very thin omelet. Cut the omelet into the required number of squares, place a little of the coriander leaves, chili slices and mixture onto each square and fold to resemble a package.

Serves 4
Preparation time: **30 mins**
Cooking time: **30 mins**

Make a cone from a piece of banana leaf or waxed or parch-ment paper.

Stir-fry all the ingredients for the chicken-shrimp mixture in a wok.

Shape the egg mixture into a square net, about 10 x 10 cm (4 x 4 in).

Fold the egg nest over the chicken-shrimp mixture, so it resembles a small package.

Golden Dumplings

3 fresh coriander roots
5 cloves garlic, minced
5 black peppercorns
$^1/_2$ lb (225 g) shrimps, finely chopped
$^1/_2$ lb (225 g) ground pork
4 oz (120 g) dried bean thread noodles, soaked in
   water 20 minutes, drained, and cut into 2-in (5-cm)
   lengths
6 water chestnuts, peeled and finely chopped
$^1/_2$ teaspoon salt
$^1/_2$ tablespoon fish sauce
3 cups (750 ml) plus 2 tablespoons oil
30 small spring roll wrappers
30 scallion leaves, blanched
Spicy-sweet Thai Dip (see page 11)

1 Grind the coriander roots, garlic and peppercorns
until fine. Transfer half of the paste to a mixing bowl.
Add the shrimps, pork, noodles, water chestnuts, salt
and fish sauce and stir well to combine.
2 Heat 2 tablespoons oil in a wok or skillet over
medium-high heat. Add the remaining garlic paste and
stir-fry until golden. Add the shrimp and pork mixture
and stir-fry for 4 or 5 minutes. Remove from the heat.
3 Place a spring roll wrapper on a flat surface and
spoon 1 tablespoon mixture onto the center of wrapper.
Gather the edges together to form a small sack. Tie
the sack with a scallion leaf and set aside. Repeat with
the remaining wrappers.
4 Heat the 3 cups oil in a wok over medium heat and
gently put the sacks in the oil, a few at a time. Cook
the sacks until golden brown. Remove with a slotted
spoon. Drain on a wire rack. Serve with Spicy-sweet
Thai Dip.

Serves 4 to 6
Preparation time: **20 mins**
Cooking time: **15 mins**

Spicy Balinese Chicken Parcels

3 tablespoons plus
2 teaspoons oil
2 tablespoons shallots,
finely chopped
1 tablespoon garlic,
minced
1 1/2 lbs (675 g) chicken
breast, coarsely chopped
1–2 fresh red chilies,
thinly sliced
1/2 cup (125 ml)
coconut milk
1/2 teaspoon salt
6–8 *salam* leaves or
3 sprigs of lemon basil
3 tablepoons tamarind
juice (see page 9)
Banana leaves for
wrapping (see page 40)

Seasoning Paste
1 tablespoon coriander
seeds
1 teaspoon black
peppercorns
4 candlenuts or
macadamia nuts
2 fresh red chilies
4 shallots
3 cloves garlic
1 stem lemongrass,
tender bottom portion
only, sliced
1 teaspoon turmeric
powder
1 in (2 1/2 cm) fresh
galangal or ginger root,
peeled
1 1/2 teaspoons palm
sugar, shaved or
crumbled
1 teaspoon salt

1 To prepare the Seasoning Paste, dry-roast the coriander seeds, peppercorns and candlenuts or macadamia nuts in a skillet until fragrant, then grind to a powder in a spice grinder or mortar and pestle. Add all other ingredients. Process until finely ground, adding a little oil if needed to keep the mixture turning.
2 Heat 3 tablespoons oil in a skillet, preferably with a nonstick surface. Add Seasoning Paste and sauté over medium heat until fragrant, about 5 minutes. Transfer to a plate and set aside to cool.
3 Heat 2 teaspoons oil in the same skillet and sauté the chopped shallots and garlic until translucent, about 2 minutes. Place in a bowl and stir in the chicken, chilies, coconut milk, salt, *salam* leaves, tamarind and cooled Seasoning Paste, mixing thoroughly.
4 Wrap and cook the packages according to the steps outlined on pages 40–41. If banana leaves are not available, dish the filling into an ovenproof baking dish, cover and steam for 15 to 20 minutes.

Serves 4
Preparation time: **40 mins**
Cooking time: **45 mins**

Double-wrapped Banana Leaf Packets (*Tum*)

The banana leaf is a very versatile cooking utensil and is widely used in Asian kitchens. It is frequently used to wrap food for grilling, steaming, or grilling directly on hot coals. Fresh banana leaves are sometimes sold in Hispanic or Asian markets, but frozen banana leaves are more readily available. Aluminum foil can be used, though it does not impart the subtle flavors that banana leaves do. Almost any type of meat, such as duck, chicken, beef and even eels, can be minced up and seasoned to make *tum*. To use, first wipe the banana leaf clean and cut it to the required size. Dip it in boiling water or heat it directly over a gas flame until it softens enough to be pliable without cracking.

Large pieces of banana leaf as main wrapper
Small strips of banana leaf for wrapping
1 quantity Spicy Balinese Chicken filling (page 38)
Wok with cover and steaming rack or steamer set

Step 1 Cut the large banana leaf wrappers into 8 x 9 in (20 x 22 cm) sheets.

Step 2 Cut the small banana leaf wrappers into 2 x 8 in (5 x 20 cm) strips.

  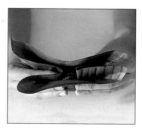

Step 3 Place 2 tablespoons of the filling in the center of a large banana leaf wrapper.

Step 4 Pleat one side of the wrapper with your index finger as you bring the two longer edges of the leaf together as shown

Step 5 Pleat the other side.

Step 6 Fold one wing of each pleat on the left and right to the front of the package.

Step 7 Fold the other wings on the other side to the back of the package.

Step 8 Place the package in the center of a smaller strip of banana leaf and fold up to hold the pleats together

Step 9 Secure with a toothpick.

Step 10 Tuck in any open corners and prepare for steaming.

Step 10 Fill a wok or steamer with about 2 in (5 cm) of water. Bring the water to a boil.

Step 11 Place the packages on the steamer rack set inside the wok or in the steamer. Cover the wok or steamer and cook for 35 minutes, adding boiling water every 10 minutes if needed. Serve hot or at room temperature.

42 Asian Noodles & Snacks

Spicy Indonesian Minced Beef Packets

1 lb (450 g) lean minced
beef
3 large eggs, lightly beaten
5–6 sour carambola,
sliced
2–3 fresh red chilies,
seeded and very thinly
sliced
8 *salam* leaves (optional)
1 cup (250 ml)
coconut cream

Spice Paste
3 teaspoons coriander
seeds
$1/2$ teaspoon cumin seeds
1 teaspoon freshly
ground black pepper
3 candlenuts or unsalted
raw macadamia nuts,
chopped
8 shallots, chopped
$1/2$ in (1 cm) galangal,
chopped
$1/2$ in (1 cm) fresh
ginger, minced
4 cloves garlic
1 tablespoon palm sugar,
crumbled or shaved
1 teaspoon salt

Wrappers
3–4 frozen banana leaf
sheets

1 Prepare Spice Paste by lightly toasting coriander and cumin seeds in a dry skillet until fragrant. Transfer to a blender and process with pepper and candlenuts and process until fine. Add shallots, galangal, ginger, garlic, sugar and salt and process until smooth, adding a little of the coconut cream, as needed.
2 Put beef in a large bowl and add the Spice Paste, eggs, carambola and chili slices. Mix thoroughly to distribute seasonings evenly.
3 Place 2 to 3 tablespoons beef, $1/2$ *salam* leaf and 2 tablespoons coconut cream in the center of a banana leaf wrapper. Wrap and steam the wrapper as described on pages 40–41.
4 Unwrap and serve hot.

Serves 4 to 6
Preparation time: **35–40 mins**
Cooking time: **20 mins**

Malaysian-style Curry Puffs

The puffs can be made with many kinds of stuffing, including potatoes, sweet potatoes and taro root. You may also substitute diced or ground beef for the chicken. If you prefer a vegetarian version of this dish, replace the meat with tofu.

$^1/_2$ lb (225 g) packet frozen puff pastry
3 cups (750 ml) oil

Stuffing
1 lb (450 g) chicken breast, diced or ground
1 teaspoon salt
1 tablespoon soy sauce
5 fresh coriander roots
$^1/_2$ teaspoon white peppercorns
5 cloves garlic
2 tablespoons oil
2 teaspoons curry powder
3 tablespoons Worcestershire sauce
1 teaspoon salt
1 cup (200 g) diced onion
$^1/_2$ lb (225 g) boiled potatoes, diced

1 Defrost puff pastry sheets at room temperature for 20 to 30 minutes, according to instructions on label.
2 To make the Stuffing, combine the chicken with the salt and soy sauce and set aside.
3 Grind the coriander roots, peppercorns and garlic until smooth using a spice grinder or mortar and pestle. Heat the oil over medium heat until hot. Add the spice paste and stir-fry 2 to 3 minutes, until fragrant. Add the meat and continue to fry until the meat changes colour. Add the curry powder, Worcestershire sauce and salt and stir well to combine.
4 Add the onion and potatoes and continue cooking until the mixture looks dry. Set aside to cool.
5 Roll out the dough and cut into circles of 4 in (10 cm) in diameter. Place 1 tablespoon Stuffing slightly off the center of each circle, fold each in half and pinch the edges shut.
5 Heat the oil in a large skillet and fry the puffs until golden, or bake at 400°F (200°C) for 12 minutes.

Makes 24
Preparation time: **45 mins**
Cooking time: **15 mins**

Place 1 tablespoon of Stuffing on the dough, slightly off-center.

After folding the circle in half, lightly pinch the edges to seal the puff.

Fried Tofu Cubes with Hot and Sweet Sauce

1 lb (450 g) firm tofu, cut into large cubes
1 cup (160 g) all-purpose flour
1 teaspoon salt
1 teaspoon freshly ground black pepper
2 large eggs, lightly beaten
2 cups (140 g) unseasoned breadcrumbs
2 cups (500 ml) oil
Sweet and Spicy Apricot Sauce (see page 9)

Serves 4
Preparation time: **40 mins**
Cooking time: **15 mins**

1 Wrap the tofu pieces in several layers of paper towels, applying light pressure to remove excess water. Set aside on dry paper towels.

2 To prepare the tofu, mix the flour, salt and pepper in a small bowl. Dredge the tofu pieces in the flour mixture, then dip into the egg mixture and coat with the breadcrumbs.

3 Heat the oil in a wok over medium-high heat. Deep-fry several pieces of tofu at a time until golden brown. Remove from the oil with a slotted spoon. Drain on paper toweling. Serve with the Sweet and Spicy Apricot Sauce.

Savory Shrimp Fritters

1 cup (125 g) all-purpose flour
1 cup (125 g) self-rising flour
1$^1/_2$ teaspoons salt
Pinch white pepper
$^1/_4$ teaspoon ground turmeric
1$^1/_2$ cups (375 ml) water, more if required
6$^1/_2$ oz (200 g) medium shrimp, peeled, deveined and
   cut in $^1/_2$-inch (1-cm) lengths
1 onion, halved lengthwise and sliced across
$^1/_2$ cup (50 g) Chinese chives or spring onion, cut into
   1$^1/_4$-in (3-cm) lengths
$^1/_4$ cup (50 g) corn kernels, (optional)
Oil for frying

1 Sift the flours together into a mixing bowl. Add the salt, pepper and turmeric and stir in enough water to make a thick batter that falls off a spoon easily. Mix with a spoon, but do not beat.
2 Stir in shrimp, onion, chives and corn kernels.
3 Heat $^3/_4$ in (2 cm) oil in a wok or saucepan. Drop heaped tablespoons of batter into the hot oil and fry until golden brown on both sides, about 4 minutes. Drain on paper towel and serve warm with chili sauce.

Serves 4
Preparation time: **20 mins**
Cooking time: **20 mins**

Thai Fish Cakes

1 lb (450 g) fresh or frozen fish fillets
$1/4$ cup (60 ml) Red Curry Paste (see page 10)
1 tablespoon fish sauce
$1/2$ teaspoon salt
1 teaspoon sugar
6 kaffir lime leaves, very thinly sliced
2 tablespoons tapioca flour or cornstarch
2 tablespoons all-purpose flour
1 egg
$1/2$ cup (100 g) winged beans or green beans,
  thinly sliced
3 cups (750 ml) oil for deep-frying
Cucumber Salad (see page 10) or Sweet and Spicy
  Apricot Sauce (see page 9)

1 Process the fish in a food processor briefly until coarsely chopped, or slice and chop finely with a large knife. Combine the fish with the Red Curry Paste, fish sauce, salt, sugar, lime leaves, tapioca flour or cornstarch and all-purpose flour in a large mixing bowl. Stir well until the mixture becomes sticky. Add the egg, stir several times, then add the beans. Mix well.
2 Heat the oil in a wok over medium-high heat. Dip your hand in water to prevent sticking, then shape 1 heaped tablespoon mixture into a patty around 2 in (5 cm) across and $1/2$ in (1 cm) thick. Carefully put each cake into the hot oil and cook until golden brown. Remove from the oil with a slotted spoon. Drain on paper toweling. Serve with Cucumber Salad or Sweet and Spicy Apricot Sauce.

Serves 4 to 6
Preparation time: **20 mins**
Cooking time: **15 mins**

Thai Crab Cakes

1 cup (125 g) fresh
crabmeat, picked clean
¹/₂ cup (80 g) ground
pork
¹/₂ cup (130 g) cooked
and mashed taro root
or potato
1 sprig fresh coriander
leaves (cilantro), finely
chopped
2 cloves garlic, minced
1 teaspoon fish sauce
1 egg, lightly beaten
¹/₂ teaspoon salt
¹/₂ teaspoon freshly
ground black pepper
4 clean crab shells
2 cups (500 ml) oil for
deep-frying

1 Combine the crabmeat, pork, taro root or potato, coriander, garlic, fish sauce, egg, salt and pepper. Fill the crab shells with this mixture.

2 Steam the shells over high heat for 15 minutes.

3 Heat the oil in a wok over high heat. Fry the shells, meat side down, until brown. Serve with Sweet and Spicy Apricot Sauce (see page 9).

If crab shells are not available, form little crab cake patties and pan fry over medium heat, 3–4 minutes on each side.

Serves 4
Preparation time: **15 mins**
Cooking time: **25 mins**

Shrimps in a Blanket

2 fresh coriander roots
1 clove garlic
$^1/_2$ teaspoon salt
6 whole peppercorns
1 teaspoon light
  soy sauce
12 medium shrimps,
  peeled and deveined,
  with tails intact
6 spring roll wrappers,
  cut in half
2 cups (500 ml) oil for
  deep-frying
1 cup (250 ml) Sweet
  and Spicy Apricot Sauce
  (see page 9)

1 Using a pestle and mortar or spice grinder, grind the coriander roots, garlic, salt and peppercorns until fine. Add the light soy sauce. Marinate the shrimps in this mixture for a few minutes.

2 Wrap each shrimp in half a spring roll wrapper, covering the body of the shrimp but leaving the tail exposed.

3 Heat the oil in a saucepan or wok over medium heat. Deep-fry the shrimps, a few at a time, until golden brown. Remove the shrimps and drain on paper toweling. Serve the shrimps with the Sweet and Spicy Apricot Sauce.

Makes 12
Preparation time: **15 mins**
Cooking time: **10 mins**

Fried Gujarati-style Potato Patties

2 slices bread
10 oz (300 g) potatoes,
  boiled and mashed
1 green chili, seeded and
  finely chopped
2 tablespoons fresh
  coriander leaves
  (cilantro), finely chopped
2 sprigs curry leaves
  (optional)
$1/4$ teaspoon ground
  turmeric
$1/2$ teaspoon chili powder
$1/2$ teaspoon salt
Oil for frying

Makes 10 patties
Preparation time: **15 mins**
Cooking time: **25 mins**

1 Dip the bread slices in water, and squeeze dry. Place the bread, potatoes, chili, coriander leaves, curry leaves, turmeric, chili powders and salt into a mixing bowl and mix thoroughly.

2 Divide the mixture into 10 balls and shape each ball into patties about $1^3/_4$ in (4 cm) round.

3 Heat the oil and fry the patties on both sides until golden brown. Remove with a slotted spoon and drain on paper towels. Serve with various chutneys (see pages 14–15).

Potato patties can also be grilled. Brush oil on both sides of the patties and grill over high heat for about 8 minutes until light brown on both sides.

Tasty Cauliflower Pakoras

1 1/2 cups (180 g) chickpea flour
2 tablespoons rice flour
1 teaspoon salt
1/2 teaspoon chili powder
1 teaspoon cumin seeds, pounded coarsely
1/2 cup (125 ml) water
1 green chili, seeded and finely chopped
1 1/2 cups (300 g) finely chopped cauliflower
1 medium onion, finely grated
2 teaspoons ginger paste
Oil for deep-frying

1 Sift the flours, salt, chili powder and cumin seeds into a mixing bowl. Make a well in the center and stir in water to make a smooth thick batter. Add chopped chili, cauliflower, onion and ginger paste to the batter, stir thoroughly.

2 Heat the oil for deep-frying. Drop tablespoons of the batter into the hot oil. Deep-fry until golden brown. Remove with a slotted spoon and drain on paper towels. Serve hot with various chutneys (see pages 14–15).

Serves 4
Preparation time: **20 mins**
Cooking time: **15 mins**

Fried Corn Patties

2 fresh coriander stems and roots
2 cloves garlic, peeled
$^1/_2$ teaspoon whole peppercorns
$^1/_2$ lb (225 g) ground pork
2 cups (300 g) fresh corn kernels or 1 10 oz (300 g)
  can corn kernels, drained
1 large egg
1 tablespoon all-purpose flour
1 tablespoon tapioca flour or cornstarch
$^1/_2$ tablespoon light soy sauce
$^1/_2$ tablespoon fish sauce
$^1/_2$ teaspoon salt
2 kaffir lime leaves, thinly sliced crosswise (optional)
2 cups (500 ml) oil
Sweet and Spicy Apricot Sauce (see page 9)

1 Using a pestle and mortar, pound the coriander roots, garlic and peppercorns until fine. Transfer to a mixing bowl. Add the remaining ingredients, except the oil and stir well.
2 Heat the oil in a wok or large skillet over medium-high heat. Shape 1 heaping tablespoon mixture into a patty. Carefully slide each patty into the oil and cook on both sides until golden brown. Remove from the oil with a slotted spoon. Drain on paper towels. Repeat until the batter is used up. Serve hot with Sweet and Spicy Apricot Sauce.

If fresh corn kernels are not available, use canned or frozen ones as substitute.

Serves 4
Preparation time: **15 mins**
Cooking time: **15 mins**

In a mixing bowl, combine all the stuffing ingredients.

Divide dough into 6 balls then, using thumb and fingers, press the dough flat into a disc.

Cauliflower-stuffed *Paratha* Flatbreads

2 cups (250 g) whole
  wheat flour
$^1/_2$ teaspoon salt
1 tablespoon oil or butter
$^3/_4$ cup (180 ml) plus
  2 tablespoons water

Filling
1 cup (250 g)
  cauliflower, finely
  chopped
2 teaspoons lemon juice
$^1/_2$ teaspoon salt
4 tablespoons fresh
  coriander leaves
  (cilantro), chopped
$^1/_2$ cup (100 g) onion,
  minced
1 green chili, thinly sliced
1 teaspoon ginger,
  grated
Oil or ghee for frying

Makes 6 *paratha*
Preparation time: **45 mins**
Cooking time: **5 mins**

1 Sift flour and salt into a large bowl and rub in the oil with your fingertips. Add the 3/4 cup (180 ml) water a bit at a time to make a soft, pliable dough, adding more water if needed. Knead until the dough is smooth and elastic, cover and set aside to rest for 30 minutes.
2 To, make the filling, put the chopped cauliflower into a bowl and add enough boiling hot water to cover. Put a lid on the bowl and set aside for 5 minutes. Drain in a sieve, pressing with a spoon to extract as much liquid as possible.
3 In a mixing bowl, combine the drained cauliflower, lemon juice, salt, coriander leaves, onion, chili and ginger. Stir thoroughly and divide into 6 portions.
4 To assemble, knead dough again and divide into 6 portions. Press a portion of the cauliflower mixture onto each disk and fold the disk over in half, pressing the edges together to close. Try not to get the edges wet or they will be difficult to close. Shape into a ball again. Press the dough flat into a disk about 5 in (12 cm) across and $^1/_4$ in ($^1/_2$ cm) thick, being careful not to break open the filling.
5 Heat oil on a griddle and fry the disks until both sides are golden brown. Serve with various chutneys (see pages 14–15).

Divide cauliflower mixture between dough disks, then pinch the edges close.

Place paratha *on a floured board and gently roll flat without breaking open.*

Fried Potato Bread

This light and delicious Indian bread puffs up when-fried, and tastes great served with various chutneys!

10 oz (300 g) potatoes, peeled
2 cups (200 g) all-purpose flour
5 tablespoons yogurt
1 teaspoon salt
6 tablespoons water
Oil for deep-frying

1 Place potatoes in a saucepan, cover with water, bring to a boil over medium heat and cook 10 to 15 minutes, or until tender. Drain, peel and mash until free of lumps.
2 Sift the flour into a bowl and add the yogurt, salt and mashed potatoes.
3 Mix by hand to form a soft dough, adding enough water to moisten the mixture. Knead for 10 minutes and set aside for 10 minutes.
4 Divide the mixture into 12 balls. Place one ball on a work surface dusted with flour. Roll out into a 4 in (10 cm) round pancake, or *puri*, with a rolling pin.
5 Heat the oil and deep-fry 1 or 2 puris at a time until they turn golden brown.
6 Remove from the oil with a slotted spoon and drain on paper towels. Serve with various chutneys (see pages 14–15).

Makes 12 pieces
Preparation time: **25 mins**
Cooking time: **20 mins**

Thai Rice Crackers with Dip

2 cups (500 ml) oil
10 to 12 puffed rice cakes (purchased)
1 dried chili, soaked 20 minutes
1 fresh coriander stem and root, minced
4 cloves garlic
1 teaspoon whole black peppercorns
1¹/₂ cups (375 ml) coconut milk
¹/₃ lb (150 g) lean ground pork
¹/₄ lb (100 g) shrimp meat, chopped
¹/₂ cup (100 g) ground roasted peanuts
1 tablespoon tomato paste
2 tablespoons palm sugar, shaved or crumbled
1 tablespoon fish sauce
¹/₂ teaspoon salt
2 tablespoons shallots, thinly sliced
1 sprig fresh coriander leaves (cilantro), roughly chopped
1 fresh chili, seeded and thinly sliced

1 Heat the oil in a wok over medium heat. Fry the rice cakes, a few at a time, until lightly golden, turning to brown both sides. Remove and set aside on paper towels to drain.

2 Grind the chili, coriander root, garlic and peppercorns until fine, using a mortar and pestle or spice grinder.

3 Heat the coconut milk in a saucepan over medium heat until it begins to boil. Add the spice mixture and stir a few times. Add the pork and shrimps and stir until well mixed. Add the peanuts and continue cooking for 5 minutes. Add the tomato paste, palm sugar, fish sauce and salt and continue to cook for 15 minutes more. The consistency should resemble chili con carne.

4 Remove the mixture from the heat and put into a serving bowl. Sprinkle with the shallots, coriander and chili. Place the bowl on a platter and surround with the rice cakes. To serve, spoon the dip over each piece of cake.

Serves 6 to 8
Preparation time: **20 mins**
Cooking time: **30 mins**

Deep-fried Crispy Crab Claws

8 large uncooked crab
claws, cracked and
cleaned
$1/_2$ lb (225 g) crab meat,
uncooked if possible
(aboout 2 cups)
6 cloves garlic, minced
2 teaspoons coriander
root or stem, minced
2 teaspoons oyster sauce
2 tablespoons fish sauce
$1/_2$ teaspoon ground
white pepper
Yolk of 2 eggs
$2/_3$ cup (50 g)
breadcrumbs
3 cups (750 ml)
vegetable or peanut oil
for deep-frying
Sweet and Spicy Apricot
Sauce (see page 9)
Lime zest from one lime

1 Try to find fresh crab claws if possible. If not, cooked crab claws may also be used. Crack the claws and carefully remove the meat reserving the claw and shells.
2 Mince the crab meat and chopped garlic, coriander root, oyster sauce, fish sauce and pepper. Add enough egg yolk to bind mixture.
3 With a small amount of oil on your hands, shape the crab meat around the claw to about 1 in ($2^1/_2$ cm) in diameter.
4 Roll the claw with the meat in the breadcrumbs. Heat the oil in a wok to medium hot, about 275 to 300°F (120 to 135°C), slowly lower the claws into the oil. Cook until golden brown, about 7 minutes. Serve with Sweet and Spicy Plum Sauce (see page 9) and zest of lime.

Serves 4
Preparation time: **20 mins**
Cooking time: **10 mins**

Add egg yolks to bind the crab, garlic, coriander root, oyster sauce and pepper.

Shape the minced crab meat around the claw of each crab to about one inch.

Roll the claw combined with the meat in the breadcrumbs.

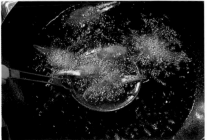

Lower the claws into the oil and cook until golden brown.

Grilled Lemongrass Chicken

Noodles and a green salad make fine partners for this delicious chicken, which you can serve as an appetiser or main course.

2 stalks lemongrass,
  thinly sliced
3 shallots, peeled and
  chopped
1 chili, chopped
3 cloves garlic, peeled
  and chopped
1 tablespoon oil
$1/4$ teaspoon salt
1 tablespoon soy sauce
1 tablespoon oyster sauce
2 teaspoons fish sauce
1 tablespoon honey
1 teaspoon sugar
1 teaspoon sesame oil
$1/4$ teaspoon freshly
  ground black pepper
1 lb (450) g chicken
  meat, cubed
12 bamboo skewers

1 Pound the lemongrass, shallots, chili, garlic and oil in a pestle and mortar until fine. Add the salt, soy sauce, oyster sauce, fish sauce, honey, sugar, sesame oil and pepper to the lemongrass mixture, stirring well to combine. Place the chicken cubes in a large mixing bowl with the paste and marinate for about 1 hour.
2 Meanwhile, soak the bamboo skewers in water so they do not catch fire.
3 Thread the chicken cubes on the skewers and grill over medium-hot coals until done, about 5 minutes on each side. Remove from the fire and serve.

Serves 3–4
Preparation time: **30 mins**
Cooking time: **8 mins**

Indonesian Chicken Satay

1 lb (450 g) chicken
   breast, cut into 1-in
   (2$\frac{1}{2}$-cm) cubes
24 bamboo skewers

Marinade
3 cloves garlic
4 shallots
1 teaspoon ground
   coriander
$\frac{1}{4}$ teaspoon ground
   cumin
$\frac{1}{2}$ teaspoon salt
3 tablespoons tamarind
   juice (see page 6)
1$\frac{1}{2}$ tablespoons oil

Peanut Sauce
2 teaspoons oil
1–2 fresh red chilies,
   sliced
3 cloves garlic, minced
1$\frac{1}{3}$ cups (200 g)
   unsalted peanuts,
   dry-roasted and skinned
$\frac{1}{2}$ teaspoon salt
3 tablespoons palm sugar,
   shaved or crumbled,
   or dark brown sugar
1 cup (250 ml) hot water

Sweet Soy Sauce Dip
2 teaspoons oil
$\frac{1}{3}$ cup (90 ml) sweet
   soy sauce
1 fresh red chili, thinly
   sliced
1 teaspoon, fresh lime
   juice

1 To make the Marinade, process garlic, shallots, coriander, cumin, salt and tamarind juice to a smooth paste in a blender. Transfer to a bowl and stir in the oil. Add the chicken cubes, mix well and set aside to marinate for at least 30 minutes.

2 To prepare the Peanut Sauce, heat the oil in a small saucepan. Cook chilies and the garlic over low to medium heat, stirring frequently until soft, about 5 minutes. Put into a food processor with the peanuts, salt and palm sugar and process briefly so that the peanuts are still chunky. Add hot water and process again briefly to make a thick sauce. Transfer to a serving bowl.

3 Thread 4 to 5 pieces of chicken cubes onto each skewer. Grill over hot charcoal or under a grill until golden brown on both sides and cooked, about 5 minutes. Serve with Peanut Sauce and Sweet Soy Sauce Dip.

If sweet Indonesian or Chinese soy sauce is not available, you may mix 2 tablespoons dark brown sugar with 6 tablespoons of thick Chinese soy sauce.

Serves 4
Preparation time: **35–40 mins**
Cooking time: **20 mins**

Thai Pork Satay

1 tablespoon thick soy
sauce
1 lb (450 g) pork loin,
cut into 1-in (2^1/$_2$-cm)
cubes
24 bamboo skewers
Coconut milk for basting

Marinade
^{1}/$_2$ cup (100 g) onion,
coarsely chopped
3 cloves garlic, peeled
1 stalk lemongrass,
tender bottom half only,
sliced
3 slices fresh ginger
1 teaspoon ground
turmeric
2 teaspoon salt
2 tablespoons tamarind
juice (see page 9)
1 tablespoon palm sugar
2 tablespoons oil
^{1}/$_3$ cup (90 ml) water, or
more as needed

Thai Peanut Sauce
2 tablespoons oil
2 tablespoons Red Curry
Paste (see page 10)
^{1}/$_2$ cup (50 g) Crispy
Fried Shallots
(see page 13)
One 13 oz (400 ml) can
coconut milk
^{1}/$_2$ cup (90 g) roasted
peanuts, coarsely ground
2 tablespoons palm sugar
or dark brown sugar
1 tablespoon tamarind
juice (see page 9)
1 teaspoon salt

1 Combine the Marinade ingredients in a blender and process until smooth. Pour the mixture into a large bowl.
2 Stir in the sweet soy sauce and add the pork cubes. Marinate the meat for at least 2 hours.
3 To make the Thai Peanut Sauce, heat the oil in a wok over high heat. Add the Red Curry Paste and fried shallots and stir until fragrant, about 3 minutes. Add the remaining ingredients and stir well. Reduce the heat to low and cook until the mixture begins to thicken; thin with some water if it gets too thick. Remove from the heat and place in a serving dish.
4 Thread 3 to 4 pieces of meat onto each skewer. Cook over a charcoal fire or under a broiler until brown. Baste each side once with coconut milk or oil while cooking. Serve with Thai Peanut Sauce and Cucumber Salad (see page 10).

Makes 24 sticks
Preparation time: **30 mins + 2 hours soaking**
Cooking time: **30 mins**

Spicy Indian Beef Kebabs

1¼ lbs (600 g) beef, cut
cut into 1-in (2½-cm)
cubes
2 tablespoons ground
cumin seeds
2 teaspoons *garam
masala*
2 teaspoons cayenne
pepper
4 tablespoons yogurt
3 tablespoons garlic,
crushed
3 tablespoons ginger,
grated
3 tablespoons papaya,
crushed (optional)
¼ cup (60 ml) vinegar
½ teaspoon salt
Oil or ghee for basting

1 Mix beef cubes together with all the ingredients
except the oil in a bowl and marinate for 4 hours.
2 Thread beef chunks on skewers until brown, and grill
over hot coals or under broiler for around 5 minutes.
3 Let stand at room temperature for 20 minutes or
longer, baste with oil or ghee and grill for another
minute before serving.

Serves 4
Preparation time: **20 mins + 4 hours standing time**
Cooking time: **15 mins + 20 mins standing time**

Fragrant Sultana Lamb Patties

1 lb (450 g) minced lean
  lamb
$^1/_3$ cup (60 g) raisins,
  chopped
1 tablespoon ground
  almonds or cashews
3 tablespoons ginger,
  grated
2 tablespoons garlic,
  crushed
1 teaspoon ground
  cardamom
1 teaspoon cayenne
  pepper
3 tablespoons chickpea
  flour
$^1/_2$ teaspoon mace
1 teaspoon salt
Oil for frying

1 Dry-roast the chickpea flour in small skillet over
medium heat until golden brown, around 3–4 minutes.
2 Combine meat and other ingredients except the oil
in a large bowl, mix well and set aside in the refrigerator
for 30 minutes.
3 Divide the mixture into 10 roughly equal portions
and roll into small patties.
4 Heat oil in a skillet over medium-low heat and cook
until both sides are light brown, about 5 minutes on
each side. Remove and drain on paper towels.

Makes 10 patties
Preparation time: **10 mins + 30 mins standing time**
Cooking time: **20 mins**

Chicken Tikka Kebabs

1 1/4 lb (600 g) chicken breast, cubed
Oil or ghee for basting
24 bamboo skewers

Marinade
4 tablespoons plain yogurt
3 tablespoons garlic, crushed
3 tablespoons ginger, grated
4 tablespoons lemon juice
1 tablespoon chickpea flour
1 teaspoon ground cumin
1/2 teaspoon ground cardamom seeds
1 teaspoon cayenne pepper
1/2 teaspoon ground turmeric
1/2 teaspoon *garam masala*
1/2 teaspoon salt

1 In a large mixing bowl, stir together all the
Marinade ingredients to form a smooth mixture. Add
the chicken cubes, mix well and leave to marinate for
3 to 5 hours in the refrigerator.
2 Skewer the chicken cubes and roast in a hot oven or
tandoor for 5 minutes. Baste with oil or ghee and roast
a further 5 minutes.

Serves 4
Preparation time: **10 mins + 3 hours standing time**
Cooking time: **20–25 mins**

Chicken Wings in Caramel Sauce

Vietnamese love the salty-sweet taste of food cooked in caramel sauce, and often use the sauce to enliven prawns, fish, pork and chicken. These tasty wings will be the hit of any meal and are ideal partners for a mild-tasting vegetable dish.

2 lbs (1 kg) chicken
wings
4 slices fresh ginger,
shredded
2/3 cup (170 ml)
Vietnamese Caramel
Sauce, (see page 12)

Serves 6–8
Preparation time: **10 mins**
Cooking time: **30 mins**

1 Separate the wings into 3 sections, reserving the tips for making chicken stock.
2 Place the chicken and ginger in a large saucepan and pour the caramel sauce over top. Bring the mixture to a boil over high heat. Cover and reduce the heat to low and cook for 30 minutes, stirring occasionally. Remove from the heat, pour off excess fat and serve.

Grilled Spareribs with Lemongrass

2 stalks lemongrass,
  thinly sliced
3 shallots, peeled and
  diced
4 cloves garlic, peeled
1 fresh or dried chili
$^1/_3$ cup (85 ml)
  Vietnamese Caramel
  Sauce, (see page 12)
2 lbs (1 kg) spareribs,
  cut into separate ribs

Serves 4–6
Preparation time:
  1 hour 10 mins
Cooking time: 30 mins

1 Pound the lemongrass, shallots, garlic and chili with a mortar and pestle or process with a food processor until fine. Stir this mixture into the Caramel Sauce.
2 Place the ribs in a large baking pan and marinate them with the Caramel Sauce for 1 hour. Preheat the oven to 350°F (180°C, gas mark 4).
3 Bake the ribs in an oven for about 20 minutes, turning over once.
4 Just before grilling, strain off the sauce and save for basting during grilling. Grill the ribs over medium-hot coals for about 10 minutes, 5 minutes on each side, or until browned. Turn often and brush with the caramel Sauce. Remove from the heat and serve immediately.

Grilled Meatballs with Vietnamese Peanut Sauce

These meatballs are equally good grilled over charcoal or broiled under an oven grill.

8 oz (225 g) dried rice vermicelli noodles
12 bamboo skewers
1 lb (450 g) lean pork or beef, cut into small pieces
2 cloves garlic, peeled and minced
$1/2$ teaspoon salt
$1/2$ teaspoon sugar
1 tablespoon rice wine
1 tablespoon Roasted Rice Powder (see page 13)
1 tablespoon fish sauce
1 tablespoon oil
1 lb (450 g) butterhead lettuce leaves
1 cup (40 g) fresh mint leaves
5 stalks fresh coriander leaves (cilantro)
1 cucumber, peeled and cut into thin strips
$1 1/2$ cups (400 g) ripe pineapple, peeled and cubed (from $1/4$ whole pineapple)
750 ml (3 cups) Vietnamese Peanut Sauce (see page 12)

1 Soak the noodles in cold water for 20 minutes. Blanch in boiling water, then rinse under cold water. Drain well and set aside on a plate. Soak the bamboo skewers in water.

2 To make the meatballs, combine the pork, garlic, salt, sugar and rice wine in a large mixing bowl. Marinate the meat for 30 minutes, then pound the meat with a mortar and pestle or grind in a food processor until fine.

3 Put the ground meat in a large mixing bowl and stir in the Roasted Rice Powder, fish sauce and oil. Mix well. Form meat into $1/2$-in (1-cm) balls and shape 2 to 3 balls around each bamboo skewer, squeezing the meat firmly so that it clings to the skewer. Repeat until meat is used up. Set aside.

4 Arrange the vermicelli, lettuce leaves, mint leaves, fresh coriander, cucumber and pineapple on a serving platter. Set aside.

5 Cook the meatballs over medium-hot coals, or alternately, broil them in the oven. Turn the skewers often to ensure the meat browns and cooks evenly. When done, remove from the heat and arrange the skewers on the platter with the vegetables.

6 To serve, pass the platter and let each person take a lettuce leaf, and place on the leaf a small portion of noodles, 1 meatball, mint leaves, fresh coriander leaves, cucumber and pineapple before folding this into a packet. Serve with peanut dipping sauce.

Serves 4–6
Preparation time: **30 mins**
Cooking time: **15 mins**

Chicken Fried with Five-spice Powder

This is one of the more renowned dishes from Sichuan, popular throughout China. It calls for no fermented seasonings, such as soy sauce or vinegar, relying entirely on the five flavors contained in the five-spice powder. This is a popular *xia jiu cai* in China, which means a dish to help get the liquor down. It is often served as a bar snack and is just as popular with children, which makes it a good choice for family meals.

12 chicken drumsticks
2 tablespoons five-spice powder
1 cup (250 ml) oil
1 bunch curly parsley, washed and drained
1–2$^{1}/_{2}$ tablespoons Sichuan pepper-salt powder (optional)
Chopped fresh coriander leaves (cilantro) or scallions as garnish

Serves 4
Preparation time: **1 hour**
Cooking time: **15 mins**

1 Wash the drumsticks and pat dry with paper towels; roll them in the ground five-spice mix until evenly coated and set aside for 1 hour.
2 Heat the oil in a wok over high heat. When the oil is hot, but not smoking, add the marinated drumsticks and fry until golden brown, turning occasionally, about 8 to 10 minutes. Remove with slotted spoon and drain on paper towels.
3 In the remaining hot oil, fry the fresh parsley sprigs until crispy, about 1 minute; remove and drain.
4 Arrange the cooked parsley sprigs around the edge of a large serving dish, then place the fried drumsticks in the center. Sprinkle evenly with the Sichuan pepper-salt powder. Garnish with coriander or scallions and serve hot.

Tandoor-roasted Chicken Fillets

4 large chicken breasts, skinned and halved, 3 deep slashes made on each side
Ghee or oil for basting

Marinade
2 teaspoons cayenne pepper
2 tablespoons lime or lemon juice
7 tablespoons heavy cream
1 cup (250 ml) plain yogurt
3 tablespoons ginger, grated
3 tablespoons garlic, crushed
1 teaspoon ground cumin
2 teaspoons *garam masala*
$1/2$ teaspoon salt
1 teaspoon freshly ground black pepper
Pinch of saffron, crushed (optional)
1 teaspoon ground turmeric

1 Squeeze the lime or lemon juice over the chicken, sprinkle the cayenne pepper over them, and rub both into the fillets. Set aside.

2 Combine all the other Marinade ingredients in a bowl and mix until smooth. Add the chicken and work the Marinade into the chicken, making sure all pieces are evenly coated. Marinate for 4 to 5 hours in the refrigerator, or overnight.

3 Preheat oven to 350°F (180°C).

4 Place chicken on a roasting pan and cook in oven for 15 minutes. Baste with ghee or oil, turn the chicken pieces over and roast the other side for another 10 minutes or until the chicken is cooked.

5 Serve with slices of various lime or sliced green chilis.

Serves 4
Preparation time: **10 mins + 7 hours standing time**
Cooking time: **25 mins**

With oiled fingers, mould the shrimp paste around the middle of the cane.

Grilled shrimp on sugar cane prior to removing the meat.

Grilled Vietnamese Shrimp Mousse on Sugar Cane

1 lb (450 g) shrimps, shelled and deveined
3 cloves garlic
3 shallots
1 teaspoon sugar
1 egg white, lightly beaten
1 tablespoon fish sauce
1 tablespoon Roasted Rice Powder (see page 13)
$1/4$ teaspoon freshly ground black pepper
2 tablespoons plus $1/4$ cup (60 ml) oil
Two 6-in (15-cm) pieces sugar cane, fresh
5 oz (150 g) rice vermicelli
Scallion Oil (see page 13)
1 tablespoon Crispy Fried Shallots (page 13)
$1^1/4$ cups (300 ml) Vietnamese Fish Sauce Dip (see page 11)

1 Process the shrimps, garlic, shallots and sugar in a food processor until the mixture becomes sticky. Stir in the egg white. Alternatively, use a mortar and pestle.
2 Add the fish sauce, rice powder, black pepper and 2 tablespoons oil to the paste and stir well to combine.
3 Peel and split the sugarcane lengthwise into quarters for a total of 8 pieces. Pour $1/4$ cup (60 ml) oil into a small dish. Oil your fingers to prevent sticking and pick up about 2 tablespoons shrimp paste. Mould it around the middle of the cane, leaving the ends exposed to serve as handles. Repeat until all the shrimp paste is used. If sugar cane is not available, form into fingers on skewers. Set aside.
4 Boil the noodles, drain well, place in a serving bowl and dress with the scallion oil and fried shallots.
5 Grill the shrimp and sugar cane pieces over a grill turning often until golden but not browned, about 5 minutes. Place on a platter.
6 Serve with Vietnamese Fish Sauce Dip or as an alternative filling for Vietnamese Salad Rolls.

Serves 4–6
Preparation time: **45mins**
Cooking time: **10 mins**

Tender Fragrant Beef Noodle Soup

5 cups (1$^1/_4$ liters) water
1 lb (450 g) fresh rice
   noodles or $^1/_2$ lb (225 g)
   dried rice sticks, soaked
   in cold water for 20
   minutes
$^1/_2$ lb (225 g) fresh bean
   sprouts
1$^1/_2$ tablespoons Garlic
   Oil (see page 13)
2 sprigs fresh coriander
   leaves (cilantro)
   roughly chopped
2 scallions, finely sliced
2 tablespoons Sweet-
   sour Chili Dip
   (see page 12)

Stock

1 lb (450 g) oxtail or
   short ribs
1 lb (450 g) stewing beef
12 cups (3 liters) water
1 onion, cleaned but left
   unpeeled
1 tablespoon thick soy
   sauce
1$^1/_2$ tablespoons fish
   sauce
2 teaspoons salt
2 tablespoons light soy
   sauce
10 cloves garlic, whole
2-in (5-cm) stick cinnamon
1 star anise
3 fresh coriander roots,
   crushed
$^1/_2$ celery root
$^1/_2$ teaspoon freshly
   ground black pepper
1 teaspoon sugar
1 in (2$^1/_2$ cm) galangal
   or ginger root, grated

1 Combine the Stock ingredients in a large stockpot and bring to a boil over medium heat. Reduce the heat to low, cover and cook until the meat is very tender, about 1$^1/_2$ hours. Add more water if necessary.
2 Meanwhile, in a large saucepan, heat 5 cups (1$^1/_4$ liters) water over medium heat. When the water boils, add the noodles, stir and cook 1 minute for fresh, 3 to 4 minutes for dried, or until tender. Drain in a colander.
3 To serve, put a portion of the noodles and bean sprouts into individual soup bowls. Add 1 cup (250 ml) of the Stock and some meat to each bowl. Sprinkle Garlic Oil, coriander leaves and scallions. Serve with Sweet-sour Chili Dip or slices of red chili.

Serves 4
Preparation time: **15 mins**
Cooking time: **2 hours**

Malaysian Shrimp Noodle Soup

3 tablespoons oil
1 lb (450 g) shrimps, shelled and deveined, tails intact (reserve heads and shells)
5 cloves garlic, chopped
1 tablespoon sugar
8 cups (2 liters) water
2 chicken thighs or drumsticks
5 oz (150 g) dried rice vermicelli, blanched for 2 minutes
8 oz (225 g) dried wheat noodles, blanched for 5 minutes
1/2 lb (225 g) bean sprouts, blanched for 2 minutes
1/2 lb (225 g) water convolvulus (*kangkong*), blanched, or spinach
2 hard-boiled eggs, shelled and quartered
3 tablespoons Crispy Fried Shallots (see page 13)

Chili Paste
5 to 10 dried chilies, cut in 2-cm (3/4-in) lengths, soaked and drained
2 fresh chilies
1 teaspoon dried shrimp paste, roasted and crumbed
5 shallots, roughly chopped
3–4 tablespoons oil
1/4 teaspoon salt
1 teaspoon sugar

1 Heat oil in a wok over high heat and add the shrimps. Stir-fry until shrimps are firm and pink. Remove from the wok and set aside.

2 Add the chopped garlic to the wok and stir-fry until golden brown. Add the shrimp shells and heads and stir-fry over high heat for 5 to 6 minutes. Sprinkle in the sugar and continue frying for 2 more minutes.

3 Pour in the water and bring to a boil. Reduce heat to low and cook for 30 to 40 minutes. Add chicken thighs to the stock and simmer for 20 minutes until chicken is cooked. Take wok off the heat. Remove chicken, place on a plate and leave to cool before stripping off the skin and shredding the meat, discarding the bones. Set aside.

4 While the shrimp stock is simmering, prepare Chili Paste. In a blender, finely grind the dried and fresh chilies, shrimp paste and shallots, adding a little water if necessary. Heat oil in a wok and fry the ground chili paste over low heat until the mixture is thick and oil separates. Add salt and sugar and take pan off the heat. Transfer to a small serving bowl.

5 Allow the stock to cool to lukewarm. Strain stock into a clean pan. You should have roughly 6 cups (1 1/2 liters) shrimp broth. Taste and adjust seasonings as necessary by adding salt, pepper or a touch of sugar. Reheat to boiling point just before serving.

6 To serve, place a portion of rice vermicelli or wheat noodles, vegetables, shrimps, shredded chicken, water convolvulus and eggs in a deep soup bowl. Ladle on the hot broth, sprinkle on a generous spoonful of fried shallots and serve immediately. Serve the Chili Paste separately in a small sauce dish.

Serves 4
Preparation time: **40 mins**
Cooking time: **1 1/2 hours**

Duck Noodle Soup

1 lb (450 g) dried rice
   sticks
2 tablespoons garlic oil
1 lb (450 g) bean sprouts,
   cleaned and blanched
   for 1 minute
Half head leaf lettuce,
   leaves separated and
   rinsed
3 scallions, thinly sliced
Freshly ground white
   pepper to taste
2 sprigs fresh coriander
   leaves (cilantro),
   chopped
$1/_4$ cup (60 ml) Sweet-
   sour Chili Dip (see
   page 12) for garnish
Crushed red chilies for
   garnish (optional)

Stock
2 whole star anise
1 small cinnamon stick
3–4 lb ($1^1/_4$–2 kg) duck-
   ling, cleaned
10 cups ($2^1/_2$ liters)
   water
5 fresh coriander roots,
   crushed
1 in ($2^1/_2$ cm) galangal
   or ginger, sliced
10 cloves garlic, crushed
1 teaspoon black
   peppercorns
2 tablespoons rock sugar
$1/_4$ cup (60 ml)
   mushroom soy
   or thick soy sauce
$1/_4$ cup (60 ml) fish sauce
1 tablespoon salt

1 To prepare the Stock, roast the star anise and the cinnamon stick in a dry skillet over medium heat until fragrant, 1 to 2 minutes. Combine the remaining Stock ingredients in a large stockpot and bring to the boil over medium heat. Reduce the heat to medium-low, cover and cook the duck until tender, but not falling apart, about $1^1/_2$ hours. Remove the duck and allow to cool. Strain the stock, discard the solids and return the stock to the pot. Skim any fat from the surface. Keep warm over low heat. Bone the duck and slice the meat into bite-sized pieces. Set aside.

2 To serve, heat the noodles in boiling water to cover until soft, about 1 minute, or heat in the microwave for 2 minutes. Drain and place a portion of noodles into individual soup bowls. Add 6 to 7 pieces duck meat, 1 teaspoon garlic oil, bean sprouts and several lettuce leaves. Garnish with scallions, pepper and fresh coriander. Add 1 cup (250 ml) broth and serve with the Sweet-sour Chili Dip or crushed red chilies.

Serves 6 to 8
Preparation time: **20 mins**
Cooking time: **1 hour 40 mins**

Chicken Noodle Soup

2 tablespoons fish sauce
$^1/_2$ lb (225 g) dried rice sticks, blanched for 2 minutes in
  boiling water and drained
$^1/_2$ lb (225 g) fresh bean sprouts, cleaned and rinsed,
  heads removed
$^1/_2$ cup (100 g) onion, thinly sliced
2 sprigs fresh coriander leaves (cilantro), roughly
  chopped
1 cup (20 g) basil (optional)
1 lime or lemon, cut into wedges

Stock
One 2–3 lb (1–1$^1/_4$ kg) chicken
6 cups (1$^1/_2$ liters) chicken stock or water
2-in (5-cm) stick cinnamon
2 scallions, cut in half
1 in (2$^1/_2$ cm) fresh ginger, grated
1 teaspoon salt
1 teaspoon sugar

1 To make the Stock, combine ingredients in a large
stockpot. Bring the mixture to the boil over medium
heat, reduce the heat to low and cook for about 1 hour.
When ready to serve, lift the chicken from the pot and
leave to cool, then shred the meat. Stir the fish sauce
into the Stock.
2 To serve, place some noodles in each soup bowl.
Garnish with the shredded chicken, bean sprouts,
onion slices, fresh coriander and basil. Add about
1 cup (250 ml) stock to each bowl. Serve each bowl
with a wedge of lime to squeeze over the top.

Serves 4 to 6
Preparation time: **20 mins**
Cooking time: **1 hour**

Spicy Penang-style Tamarind Laksa

1 lb (450 g) mackerel or red snapper, cleaned
1 in (2¹/₂ cm) fresh ginger, grated
¹/₂ cup (120 ml) Tamarind Juice (see page 9)
1 teaspoon salt
6 cups (1¹/₂ liters) water
2 torch ginger buds, quartered lengthwise
5 sprigs mint
2 teaspoons salt
3 tablespoons sugar
10 oz (300 g) dried laksa noodles or rice sticks or 1 lb (450 g) fresh laksa noodles

Spice Mix
3 dried chilies, soaked in warm water for 20 minutes and chopped
2 fresh chilies, chopped
5 shallots, chopped
2 stalks lemongrass, bottom 4 in (10 cm) only, thickly sliced
2 teaspoons dried shrimp paste, toasted and crumbled

Garnish
1 small cucumber, julienned
1 cup (200 g) fresh pineapple, julienned
1 medium shallot, thinly sliced
1 torch ginger bud, thinly sliced
1 cup (40 g) mint leaves
1 red chili, seeded and thinly sliced

1 Place fish, ginger, tamarind juice and salt into a pan and cover with 4 cups (1 liter) water. Bring to a boil and reduce the heat to low. Cover pan and poach fish until cooked, about 15 minutes. Remove pan from heat. When the fish is cool enough to handle, remove from poaching liquid and remove bones. Set aside. Strain fish stock and discard bones, reserving the stock.
2 To make the Spice Mix, place dried and fresh chilies, shallots, lemongrass and shrimp paste in a blender and add enough water to process until smooth.
3 Place spice mix into a large pan and add reserved fish stock and the remaining 2 cups (500 ml) water. Add the torch ginger buds, mint, salt and sugar. Bring to a boil, reduce heat to low and cook for 30 minutes. Add the fish and cook another 15 minutes. Taste and adjust seasonings.
4 Put a large pan of water to boil and cook the dried laksa noodles for 5 to 7 minutes or until tender. If using fresh laksa noodles, blanch in hot water for 1 to 2 minutes. Drain noodles in a colander and run tap water over them to remove excess starch. Drain well before transferring to a serving dish.
5 To serve, place a portion of noodles in a deep bowl and ladle in the hot mixture. Top with the shredded cucumber and pineapple, shallot, torch ginger slices, mint leaves and chilies and serve with Shrimp Paste Dip (*hae ko*) (see page 12).

Serves 4
Preparation time: **40 mins**
Cooking time: **1 hour 45 mins**

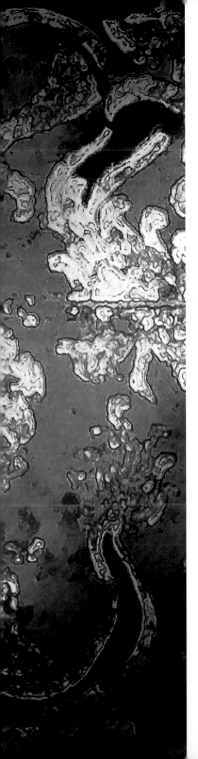

Thai Glass Noodle Soup

$1/2$ lb (225 g) lean ground pork
3 cloves garlic, minced
$1/2$ teaspoon ground white pepper
1 teaspoon salt
$1/4$ cup (60 ml) water
6 cups ($1 1/2$ liters) chicken stock
5 oz (150 g) dried bean thread noodles, soaked in
   water for 15 minutes, drained and cut into 2-in (5-
   cm) lengths
4 dried *shiitake* or wood ear mushrooms, soaked in
   hot water for 20 minutes, drained stems removed
   and thinly sliced
1 cup (120 g) chopped celery with young leaves
2 tablespoons fish sauce
1 teaspoon sugar
2 scallions, finely sliced
2 sprigs fresh coriander leaves (cilantro), chopped
Fried Garlic (see page 6) for garnishing

1 In a mixing bowl, combine the pork, garlic, pepper
and $1/2$ teaspoon of the salt and mix well by hand,
adding water as required.
2 Heat the chicken stock in a large saucepan over
medium heat. When it boils, stir in the pork and
return the stock to a boil. Simmer for 10 minutes.
3 Add the noodles, mushrooms and celery and season
with the fish sauce, remaining salt and sugar.
4 Ladle the soup, pork and noodles into individual
serving bowls and garnish with scallions, coriander
leaves and Fried Garlic.

Serves 4 to 6
Preparation time: **30 mins + 30 mins soaking**
Cooking time: **10 mins**

Fresh Pineapple Shrimp Noodles

$^1/_2$ lb (225 g) dried ramen or other wheat noodles

$^1/_2$ cup (125 ml) coconut milk

$^1/_2$ lb (225 g) medium shrimps, shelled and deveined

1 cup (300 g) crushed pineapple, preferably fresh

1 scallion, thinly sliced

Dressing

$^1/_4$ cup (60 ml) fresh lime or lemon juice

$^1/_4$ cup (60 ml) fish sauce

2 tablespoons sugar

3 cloves garlic, minced

2 tablespoons fresh ginger, grated

1 To make the Dressing, combine the lime juice, fish sauce, sugar, garlic and ginger in a mixing bowl and stir well. Set aside.

2 Cook the noodles in boiling water for 3 minutes. Drain in a colander and rinse the noodles under cold water.

3 Heat the coconut milk in a saucepan over medium heat and when it begins to simmer, add the shrimps and cook until just pink, about 3 minutes.

4 Arrange the noodles on a serving platter. Top with the shrimps and and pineapple and drizzle with the dressing. Garnish with scallion before serving.

Serves 4
Preparation time: **15 mins**
Cooking time: **10 mins**

Grilled Lemongrass Beef Noodle Salad

This one-dish salad has the advantage of being both delectable and easy to make. You can prepare and assemble everything ahead of time, making this a perfect company meal. Partially freezing the beef firms it and makes for easier slicing. If you wish, you can substitute chicken breast for the beef.

8 oz (225 g) dried rice vermicelli
1 lb (450 g) beef sirloin, flank steak or top round
1/2 cup (100 g) onion, peeled and minced
3 cloves garlic, peeled
2 stalks lemongrass, fincly chopped
1 teaspoon salt
1/2 teaspoon freshly ground black pepper
1/2 teaspoon curry powder, optional
1 tablespoon fish sauce
12 bamboo skewers
2 cups (200 g) shredded lettuce
1 cucumber, peeled and shredded
1/2 lb (225 g) bean sprouts
1 cup (40 g) fresh mint leaves
1 cup (40 g) fresh coriander leaves (cilantro), chopped
1 cup (150 g) shredded carrot
3 tablespoons oil
1/2 cup (100 g) roasted peanuts, ground
250 ml (1 cup) Vietnamese Fish Sauce Dip (see page 11)

1 Soak the noodles in cold water for 20 minutes. In a large covered saucepan, bring water to a boil and add the noodles. Cook in boiling water for 2 minutes, rinse under cold water, drain and set aside.

2 Slice the beef into thin strips and place the strips in a non-reactive container.

3 To make the marinade paste, grind the onion, garlic and lemongrass in a mortar and pestle or spice grinder. Add in the salt, black pepper, curry powder if desired, and fish sauce. Stir mixture over the beef and marinate for 1 hour.

4 Meanwhile, start the barbecue fire and soak the bamboo skewers in water.

5 Arrange the lettuce leaves, cucumber, bean sprouts, mint leaves, fresh coriander and shredded carrot on a serving platter.

6 When you are ready to eat, thread the meat strips onto the bamboo skewers. Cook over medium-hot coals, 1 to 2 minutes per side, taking care not to burn the meat. Remove the skewers from the fire and arrange the skewers on the serving platter.

7 To serve, place a portion of noodles in a large soup bowl. Then place the beef, lettuce, cucumber, bean sprouts, mint leaves, fresh coriander, carrot, and 1 teaspoon crushed peanuts on top of the noodles. Dress the ingredients with 2 tablespoons Vietnamese Fish Sauce Dip, or more to taste. Toss the ingredients together and serve. Repeat the process for each serving.

Serves 6
Preparation time: **45 mins**
Cooking time: **15 mins**

Fragrant Noodles
with Chili and Sesame Sauce

1 teaspoon salt
8 oz (225 g) dried ramen
  or other wheat noodles,
1 tablespoon sesame oil
2 baby cucumbers,
  seeded and sliced
  thinly into long, thin
  strips
1 green bell pepper,
  seeded and slivered
1 handful fresh mung
  bean sprouts, blanched
1 pickled bamboo shoot,
  blanched and julienned
1 small onion, halved and
  thinly sliced
2 tablespoons black
  sesame seeds, toasted

Sauce
2 teaspoons red chili oil
2 tablespoons dark
  sesame paste or tahini
  blended with 2 table-
  spoons water
1 tablespoon sesame oil
2 teaspoons sugar
1 tablespoon vinegar
1 teaspoon salt

1 In a large mixing bowl, stir all the Sauce ingredients together and blend until smooth. Set aside.
2 Bring a large pot of water with salt to a boil and cook the noodles according to package directions.
3 Drain the noodles, rinse under cool water and drain again well. Place noodles in a large bowl and drizzle with the sesame oil. Toss to coat evenly.
4 Add the vegetables to the sauce in the mixing bowl and toss to mix well with noodles. Place on a serving platter, or divide into individual portions in small bowls and sprinkle with toasted black sesame seeds.

Serves 4
Preparation time: 25 mins
Cooking time: 20 mins

Noodles with Meat Sauce

8 oz (225 g) dried rice sticks, soaked in hot water for
  20 minutes and drained
1 tablespoon thick soy sauce
1 teaspoon curry powder
2 tablespoons cornstarch
2 tablespoons fish sauce
$^1/_2$ lb (225 g) lean ground beef
4 tablespoons oil
4 cups (80 g) Boston lettuce, torn
3 cloves garlic, minced
$1^1/_2$ cups (375 ml) chicken or beef stock
2 sprigs fresh coriander leaves (cilantro), chopped

1 Drain the noodles well, place in a bowl, separate
them and sprinkle with the thick soy sauce. Set aside.
2 Combine the curry powder, cornstarch and fish
sauce in a mixing bowl. Stir in the ground beef and
set aside.
3 Heat 3 tablespoons of the oil in a wok over medium
heat. Stir in the noodles and cook for 3 to 4 minutes,
or until heated through. Line a serving platter with the
lettuce leaves and place the noodles on top.
4 Add the remaining oil to the wok and stir-fry the
garlic until brown. Add the beef and stir-fry for 2 to 3
minutes. Stir in the stock. Pour the meat mixture over
the noodles and garnish with the fresh coriander leaves.

Serves 2
Preparation time: **15 mins**
Cooking time: **10 mins**

Bean Sprout Noodles

The sauce may be blended to suit anyone's personal taste and virtually any type of wheat noodle may be used. Moreover, sesame is a rich source of vegetable protein, minerals and other vital nutrients.

12–16 cups (3–4 liters) water
1/2 lb (225 g) dried wheat noodles, or 1 lb (450 g) fresh noodles
1 1/2 cups (150 g) fresh mung bean sprouts, washed and drained

Sauce
3 tablespoons sesame paste or tahini
1 teaspoon salt
1 teaspoon sugar
1 tablespoon soy sauce
1 teaspoon vinegar
1 teaspoon freshly ground black pepper
4 scallions, finely sliced

1 Bring the water to a rolling boil; do not add salt.
2 Add the noodles to the water and cook dried noodles according to package directions, or about 30 seconds for fresh. Test to make sure they are tender before removing from the pot.
3 Drain noodles in a colander, rinse in cold water, drain and place in a large bowl.
4 Combine Sauce ingredients and add the Sauce to the noodles. Toss well to mix thoroughly.
5 Place portions into individual serving bowls, garnish with bean sprouts and serve.

For garnish, you may also use shreds of cucumber and carrot. For those who like it hot, add 1 tablespoon of chili sauce or 1 teaspoon of crushed red pepper to the sauce, or sprinkle crushed red pepper onto individual servings.

Serves 4
Preparation time: **15 mins**
Cooking time: **30 mins**

Tangy Malaysian Tamarind Noodles with Shrimp

2 cups (500 ml) coconut milk
$^1/_4$ cup (60 ml) yellow bean paste or miso
$^1/_4$ cup (30 g) shallots, sliced
1 tablespoon tomato paste or ketchup
$^1/_3$ cup (150 g) lean ground pork
$^1/_4$ cup (50 g) sugar
$^1/_4$ cup (60 ml) tamarind juice (see page 9)
3 tablespoons fish sauce
$^3/_4$ lb (375 g) fresh shrimps, shelled and roughly chopped, to yield 1 cup (175 g)
1 lb (450 g) dried rice vermicelli, soaked in water for 30 minutes and drained
$^1/_2$ lb (225 g) fresh bean sprouts, cleaned and heads removed
1 cup (40 g) snipped garlic chives
1 tablespoon oil
2 large eggs, lightly beaten (optional)

1 Heat the coconut milk in a wok over high heat. When it boils, add the yellow bean paste, shallots, tomato paste and ground pork. Stir well to combine. Reduce heat to medium and cook until the mixture comes to the boil.

2 Stir in the sugar, tamarind juice and fish sauce, making sure to break up any clumps of meat, then add the shrimps and cook until they turn pink. Stir in the vermicelli, mix well and continue cooking until the sauce is absorbed, about 2–3 minutes. If the vermicelli do not soften completely, stir in some water and cook a little longer. Turn off heat. Stir in the bean sprouts and garlic chives and mix them well. Remove to a serving platter.

3 Heat the oil in a skillet over medium-high heat. Stir in the eggs and cook through until firm without stirring. Slide the omelette from the pan and cut into thin shreds. Garnish the vermicelli with the egg shreds. Serve hot.

Serves 4 to 6
Preparation time: **10 mins**
Cooking time: **20 mins**

Thai Chicken Curry Noodles

2 1/2 cups (625 ml) coconut milk
1 lb (450 g) boneless chicken, cut into bite-sized pieces
2 tablespoons fish sauce
1/2 teaspoon salt
1/2 teaspoon sugar
2 cups (500 ml) oil
1 lb (450 g) dried egg noodles
1 scallion, finely chopped
1 sprig fresh coriander leaves (cilantro), chopped
1 large lime or lemon, cut in wedges

Curry Paste
2 teaspoons coriander seeds
1/2 teaspoon caraway seeds
2 dried chilies
1/2 cup (100 g) onion, peeled and sliced
6 cloves garlic
5 thin slices fresh ginger
3 cardamom pods, the inner seeds only
1/2 teaspoon ground nutmeg
1/4 teaspoon ground mace
3 whole cloves

2 teaspoons curry powder
1/2 teaspoon dried or wet shrimp paste
1/4 cup (60 ml) water, or more as needed

If preferred, beef may be used as a substitute for chicken meat. Cook for about 50 minutes.

Serves 4
Preparation time: **20 mins**
Cooking time: **25 mins**

1 To make the Curry Paste, roast the coriander and caraway seeds in a dry skillet over medium heat until fragrant, about 2 minutes. Combine with all the remaining ingredients in a blender and process until smooth, adding water as needed.

2 In a large saucepan or wok, heat 1 1/2 cups (375 ml) of the coconut milk over medium heat. When it comes to the boil, stir in the curry paste and cook until fragrant, about 5 minutes.

3 Add the chicken and stir well to mix. When the curry comes to the boil again, add the remaining coconut milk, fish sauce, salt and sugar. Cover, reduce heat to low and cook until the chicken is tender, about 20 minutes.

4 Heat the oil in a large wok over medium heat. Fry about 1/4 lb (100 g) of the noodles until golden brown. Remove with a slotted spoon. Drain on paper toweling and set aside for garnish.

5 Cook the remaining noodles in boiling water until tender, about 3 minutes. Drain and arrange the noodles in individual serving bowls.

6 To serve, pour the curry into a large tureen. Ladle the sauce over the top of each portion. Garnish each serving with the fried noodles, scallions and coriander leaves. Squeeze a wedge of lime over the top before eating.

Braised Bean Threads with Shrimp in Claypot

8 oz (225 g) dried bean thread noodles, soaked 20
   minutes, drained and cut into 2-in (5-cm) lengths
$^1/_2$ lb (225 g) medium shrimps, shelled and deveined
1 sprig fresh coriander leaves (cilantro), chopped, for
   garnish
4 cloves garlic, crushed
3 fresh coriander roots, crushed
1 in ($2^1/_2$ cm) fresh ginger, grated
1 teaspoon freshly ground black pepper
1 cup (250 ml) Basic Chicken Stock (see page 13)
2 tablespoons oil
1 tablespoon oyster sauce
1 tablespoon thick soy sauce

1 Line a claypot or casserole dish with the garlic, coriander roots, ginger and black pepper. Arrange the noodles
on top. Put the shrimps on top of the noodles.
2 Pour the Basic Chicken Stock, oil, oyster sauce and
thick soy sauce over the shrimps and noodles. Cover
and cook the mixture over high heat until the shrimps
turn pink, about 5 minutes. Garnish with the coriander
leaves and serve from the claypot or casserole dish.

Serves 4
Preparation time: **10 mins**
Cooking time: **5 mins**

Noodles with Beef and Vegetables

Leftover vegetables — and fresh ones, of course — complement the noodles in this meal-in-a-bowl.

1 lb (450 g) dried rice vermicelli

8 oz (225 g) beef, thinly sliced

4 cloves garlic, minced

5 tablespoons oil

$^1/_2$ teaspoon sugar

$^1/_2$ teaspoon salt

$^1/_4$ teaspoon freshly ground black pepper

1 large onion, halved lengthways and julienned

4 scallions, cut into 1-in (2$^1/_2$-cm) lengths

2 celery stalks, thinly sliced

1 carrot, cleaned and shredded

1 cup (120 g) broccoli florets, or cauliflower

10 large fresh mushrooms, thinly sliced

2 tablespoons soy sauce

4 tablespoons fish sauce

2 cups (500 ml) Basic Chicken Stock (see page 13)

4 tablespoons oyster sauce

1 Soak the noodles in water for 20 minutes. Drain in a colander and set aside.

2 Put the beef in a large mixing bowl and stir in the garlic, 1 tablespoon of the oil, sugar, salt and pepper. Set aside.

3 Heat 2 tablespoons of the oil in a wok over high heat. Add the beef and stir-fry for 2 to 3 minutes. Remove from the heat.

4 Add the remaining 2 tablespoons oil to the wok. When the oil is hot but not smoking, add the onion, scallions, celery, carrot, broccoli and mushrooms, stirring to mix well.

5 Stir in the soy sauce, fish sauce, 1$^1/_2$ cups (375 ml) of the chicken stock, and oyster sauce. Stir in the noodles, making sure these absorb the liquid and become soft. Add the remaining $^1/_2$ cup (125 ml) of stock if the noodles look dry. Return the beef to the wok and stir-fry 2 minutes more. Remove from the heat and serve on a large platter.

Serves 6–8
Preparation time: **20 mins**
Cooking time: **15 mins**

Classic Pad Thai Noodles

4 tablespoons oil
2 tablespoons garlic, minced
3 tablespoons tiny dried shrimps
1 tablespoon salted turnip, chopped
$^1/_2$ lb (225 g) pork loin, thinly sliced
8 oz (225 g) small shrimps, cleaned and shelled to yield $^1/_2$ cup (90 g)
1 lb (450 g) dried rice stick noodles, soaked in water 20 minutes and drained
2 large eggs
1–2 small chilies, ground
$^1/_2$ cup (20 g) garlic chives, sliced
2 tablespoons ground roasted peanuts
$^1/_2$ lb (225 g) bean sprouts, rinsed
Fresh lime juice to taste

Sauce
1 cup (250 ml) tamarind juice (see page 9)
1 cup (250 g) palm sugar, shaved and crumbled (if unavailable, use dark brown sugar and add 2 tablespoons coconut milk)
1 cup (250 ml) water
$^1/_2$ cup (125 ml) fish sauce

1 To make the Sauce, mix all ingredients in a saucepan and simmer for about 45 minutes until well mixed and syrupy, stirring occasionally. Store any leftovers in the refrigerator in a tightly sealed container.

2 Heat oil in a wok over medium to high heat. Add the garlic and stir-fry until golden brown. Add the dried shrimp and salted turnip and stir a few times. Add the pork and shrimps and stir until the shrimps change color. Remove shrimps to prevent over cooking and set aside.

3 Add the noodles to the wok. They will stick together so stir quickly to separate them. Add $^1/_2$ cup (125 ml) Sauce and keep stirring until everything is thoroughly mixed. Add more sauce as desired. The noodles should appear soft and moist. If they look hard, add a little more Sauce or water and stir again. Return the cooked shrimps to the wok.

4 Push the contents of the wok up around the sides to make room for the eggs. If the pan is very dry, add 1 tablespoon oil. Add the eggs and cover with the noodles. When the eggs are cooked, stir the noodles until everything is mixed — there should be cooked bits of egg white and yolk throughout the noodle mixture.

5 Mix in the chilies, garlic chives and half the bean sprouts. Remove to a platter. Sprinke with ground peanuts and remaining raw bean sprouts and a few drops of fresh lime juice.

This recipe calls for a dark and sweet tamarind-based sauce which gives the noodles their amber color. Don't take any shortcuts or omit any ingredients. If you plan to make this for company, cook the noodles ahead and add bean sprouts and garlic chives when you reheat the noodles. Salted or preserved turnip is sold in cellophane packets at Asian markets.

Serves 2
Preparation time: **15 mins**
Cooking time: **10 mins**

Quick Thai Basil Rice Sticks with Shrimps

Fresh wide rice noodles are commonly sold at Asian markets, though dried noodles may also be used. These are best when freshly made, but older noodles can be freshened by plunging them into boiling water to soften. Look for thick sweet soy sauce. If thick sweet soy sauce is unavailable, add 1 teaspoon brown sugar to the recipe and use normal soy sauce.

4 tablespoons oil
$^1/_2$ lb (225 g) shrimps, shelled and deveined
3 cloves garlic, minced
1 lb (450 g) fresh wide rice noodles or 10 oz (300 g) dried rice sticks
1 tablespoon thick sweet soy sauce
2 tablespoons fish sauce
1 tablespoon oyster sauce
20 basil leaves
$^1/_2$ lb (225 g) bean sprouts, cleaned and rinsed
2 dried chilies, crushed (optional)

1 If using dried rice sticks, soak for 20 minutes in water, drain and set aside.
2 Heat 1 tablespoon of the oil in a large wok over medium heat and stir-fry the shrimps for 1 to 2 minutes, or until the shrimps turn pink. Remove the shrimps and set aside.
3 Add the remaining oil to the pan and increase the heat to high. Add the garlic and cook for 20 seconds, then add the noodles and stir-fry for 2 to 3 minutes. Stir in the thick sweet soy sauce or normal soy sauce and brown sugar. Return the shrimps to the pan and stir in the fish sauce, oyster sauce, basil, bean sprouts and chilies. Place on a serving platter. Serve hot.

Serves 4
Preparation time: **10 mins**
Cooking time: **10 mins**

Stir-fried Rice Sticks with Vegetables

3 tablespoons oil
3 cloves garlic, minced
$1/2$ lb (225 g) beef, pork
   or chicken, thinly sliced
$1/2$ lb (225 g) dried rice
   stick noodles, soaked
   in water 20 minutes
   and drained
$1/2$ cup (125 ml) chicken
   stock
2 cups (200 g) cabbage,
   shredded
$1/2$ lb (225 g) bean
   sprouts, cleaned
1 cup (120 g) broccoli,
   or *bok choy*, chopped
2 scallions, cut into
   1-in ($2^1/2$-cm) lengths
$1/4$ cup (60 ml)
   Sweet-sour Chili Dip
   (see page 12)

Sauce
1 tablespoon yellow
   bean paste
1 tablespoon fish sauce
1 tablespoon thick soy
   sauce
1 tablespoon oyster
   sauce
1 teaspoon sugar

1 To make the Sauce, combine the ingredients in a small bowl and set aside.

2 Heat the oil in a wok over medium-high heat. Stir-fry the garlic until light brown, 2 to 3 minutes. Add the meat and stir-fry until it cooks through, 2 to 3 minutes.

3 Add the noodles and the Sauce. Stir to mix well. Add the stock and all the vegetables. Stir-fry until noodles are moist and soft, about 3 minutes.

4 Spoon the mixture onto a serving platter. Serve with Sweet-sour Chili Dip, as desired.

Meat leftovers or firm tofu or tofu skin can be substituted for fresh meat.

Serves 4
Preparation time: **10 mins**
Cooking time: **10 mins**

Southern Thai Rice Noodles with Beef and Broccoli

2 shallots
2 dried chilies
$1/_2$ cup (125 ml) coconut milk
$1/_2$ cup (125 ml) water
1 lb (450 g) fresh wide rice noodles
$1/_2$ lb (225 g) beef, thinly sliced
1 lb (450 g) Chinese broccoli or Western broccoli,
   stems peeled and sliced
$1/_4$ cup (60 ml) tamarind juice (see page 9)
2 tablespoons sugar
2 tablespoons thick soy sauce
4 tablespoons fish sauce

1 Using a pestle and mortar or food processor, grind the shallots and chilies until smooth.
2 Heat the coconut milk and water in a large wok over medium heat until it comes to the boil. Add the shallot mixture and cook, stirring, for 2 to 3 minutes.
3 Add the noodles, beef, Chinese broccoli, tamarind juice, sugar, sweet soy sauce and fish sauce and stir to combine. Remove to a serving platter. Serve hot.

Serves 4
Preparation time: **10 mins**
Cooking time: **10 mins**

Cantonese Fried Noodles

1/2 cup (125 ml) oil
3 1/2 oz (100 g) dried rice vermicelli, broken into small pieces
12 oz (375 g) dried rice sticks, soaked in water for 20 minutes and drained
2 tablespoon light soy sauce
2 cloves garlic, minced
5 thin slices fresh ginger
1/2 cup (60 g) carrots, thinly sliced
1/2 lb (225 g) chicken breast, thinly sliced
1/2 lb (225 g) medium shrimps, shelled and deveined
1/3 lb (150 g) fresh squid, sliced into strips
Salt and pepper to taste
4 cups (200 g) mustard greens or *bok choy*, washed and sliced
6 dries or fresh *shiitake* mushrooms (if using dried mushrooms, soak in hot water for 20 minutes), stems removed and sliced
4 cups (1 liter) Basic-Chicken Stock, (see page 13)
1 tablespoon oyster sauce
1 teaspoon sugar
2 tablespoons cornstarch mixed with 1/2 cup (125 ml) water
1 large egg, beaten
Seasoned Sliced Chilies (see page 10)

1 Heat oil in a wok over medium heat. Place a small handful of rice vermicelli and fry for a few seconds until puffed up but still pale. Remove immediately and place onto a paper-lined colander to drain the oil. Fry all the vermicelli this way and set aside.

2 Remove all but 3 tablespoons of oil from the wok. Reheat oil and fry the rice noodles over high heat for 3 to 4 minutes. Drizzle in 1 tablespoon of the light soy sauce. To serve, divide the noodles and vermicelli into four portions, placing them in individual plates or bowls.

3 Heat 2 tablespoons oil in a large saucepan and fry the garlic and ginger until golden brown. Add the sliced carrots, chicken, shrimps and squids, stir-frying quickly over high heat for 3 to 4 minutes. Season with salt and pepper. Add mustard greens and mushrooms and cook for a few minutes.

4 Pour in hot chicken stock and season with oyster sauce, the remaining light soy sauce and sugar. Thicken by stirring in the cornstarch mixture. Slowly pour in the beaten egg, allowing the mixture to bubble and cook undisturbed for 2 to 3 minutes. Remove from the heat.

5 Ladle a generous portion of gravy over the noodles and serve immediately, accompanied with each serving of Seasoned Sliced Chilies.

Serves 6
Preparation time: **30 mins**
Cooking time: **20 min**

Hainanese Fried Noodles

12 oz (375 g) dried wheat noodles, soaked in hot
  water for 20 minutes and drained
2 tablespoons oil
4 cloves garlic, minced
$1/4$ lb (100 g) chicken breast, thinly sliced
$1/4$ lb (100 g) medium shrimps, shelled and deveined
$1/4$ lb (100 g) fish cakes or fish fillets or dried tofu,
  thinly sliced
4 cups (200 g) mustard greens or *bok choy*, cut in
  2-in (5-cm) lengths
2–3 tablespoons Crispy Fried Shallots (see page 13)
  (optional)
1–2 fresh red chilies, thinly sliced

Gravy
1 tablespoon light soy sauce
$1/2$ tablespoon thick soy sauce
$1/2$ tablespoon oyster sauce
1 teaspoon sugar
$1/2$ teaspoon salt
$1/4$ teaspoon freshly ground pepper
$3/4$ cup (200 ml) water

1 To make the Gravy, stir together all the Gravy ingredients and set aside.
2 Heat oil in a wok over high heat and fry garlic until
golden brown. Add the chicken slices and stir-fry,
then add shrimps and fish cakes, or fish fillets or tofu.
Stir-fry for 3 minutes and add the greens. Toss until
wilted, about 2 minutes.
3 Pour in the Gravy, bring to the boil and add the
noodles. Reduce the heat to medium and cook for
3 to 5 minutes. Remove from the heat and transfer
onto a serving platter or four individual
serving plates. Garnish with fried shallots and serve
immediately. Serve sliced chilies separately.

Serves 4
Preparation time: **20 mins**
Cooking time: **20 mins**

Complete Recipe List